JUDAISM AND CHRISTIANITY

JUDAISM AND CHRISTIANITY:

A CONTRAST

RABBI STUART FEDEROW

iUniverse, Inc.
Bloomington

Judaism and Christianity
A Contrast

iUniverse books may be ordered through booksellers or by contacting:

iUniverse
1663 Liberty Drive
Bloomington, IN 47403
www.iuniverse.com
1-800-Authors (1-800-288-4677)

Because of the dynamic nature of the Internet, any web addresses or links contained in this book may have changed since publication and may no longer be valid. The views expressed in this work are solely those of the author and do not necessarily reflect the views of the publisher, and the publisher hereby disclaims any responsibility for them.

Any people depicted in stock imagery provided by Thinkstock are models, and such images are being used for illustrative purposes only.
Certain stock imagery © Thinkstock.

ISBN: 978-1-4759-5472-2 (sc)
ISBN: 978-1-4759-5473-9 (hc)
ISBN: 978-1-4759-5471-5 (ebk)

Library of Congress Control Number: 2012918599

Printed in the United States of America

iUniverse rev. date: 10/18/2012

CONTENTS

PART I
A Contrast of Beliefs

PART II
A Contrast in the Interpretation of the Hebrew Scriptures

To

Marcy Powers

Libbi Federow

Peri Federow

and

In Memory Of
Lisa Ann Federow, z'l

PREFACE

I saw her get out of her car with her Bible, after she drove behind me into the parking lot of the bookstore. I had seen in my rear view mirror that she stared with a look of both disdain and fascination at my Jewish bumper stickers and the appears-like-chrome-but-made-of-plastic Star of David. I held the door open for her after waiting for her to catch up to me. She thanked me, and then, hesitating as she walked in, asked me if she could talk to me.

"Great," I thought, "here we go again." But I said to her, "Sure. Is everything okay?"

"Of course, but I saw your bumper stickers. I have some questions about Judaism. Are you Jewish?"

I said, "Yes I am a Jew. Would you like to sit down and talk?"

We found some chairs and sat down. Her face showed a mix of emotions. She looked excited, even as she looked a little scared, unsure and confused, as if in a new area of town where she knew where she wanted to go, but didn't know the way to get there.

"What's on your mind?" I asked to help her begin.

She replied, "Well, I have been reading my Bible and speaking to some friends of mine who are Jewish people and I have been reading a few books by Jewish rabbis, so I had some questions."

"Okay." I told her. "By the way, it's okay to call us 'Jews,' rather than 'Jewish People.' After all, you wouldn't say, 'a Christian person,' you would just say 'a Christian,' so just say 'a Jew,' or 'Jews,' because that's what we are."

"Really?" she said, "Because I thought it was kind of, you know, insulting to be called a Jew."

"It's only insulting to those who think there is something wrong with being a Jew," I said. Before she could protest that she didn't think there was anything wrong with being a Jew, because her best friends were Jews, I asked her, "What's your first question?"

It didn't work. She smiled and quickly said, "I want you to know that I love the Jews, and I pray for the State of Israel every day." Then her questions just spilled out. "But I don't understand why you're not all Messianic Jews? If the only thing that separates us is Jesus—we say he was the messiah and you don't—what is stopping you from accepting him? I've heard Jewish rabbis calling Jesus a rabbi, and everyone speaks of the Judeo-Christian Tradition, so if the first Christians were Jews, and Judaism just led right into Christianity, why are so many Jewish people, thousands of years later, still not accepting him?"

In response, I said, "Well, I am glad that you love the Jews and support Israel. However, I would be happier if you loved the Judaism that makes me a Jew, and support my choice of Judaism that keeps me a Jew." At that her smile disappeared, and, over the course of our conversation, it became more and more of a frown.

In many ways, this book is my response to the many questions, shallow understandings, and misrepresentations of Judaism, reflected in what she said that day. It also is my response to what others have said to me over the years, which seem to pervade our Christianity-influenced society.

I have been defending Judaism to Christians my whole life. I have been explaining what Jews believe to non-Jews since I was in early grade school. As the only Jew in grade school growing up in Springfield, Missouri, I was always asked to explain our holidays to the class, to bring Jewish ritual items for show-and-tell, and to answer the questions of friends about what we believe and why. Through High School, I was the target of friends who, to help validate their own beliefs and out of concern for me, attempted to convert me to Christianity.

These experiences growing up led me to study Comparative Religion. I majored in Religious Studies at Brown University, and was ordained a rabbi. I wrote pamphlets teaching Jews how to respond to the efforts of Christian missionaries. I wrote the chapter, 'Missionaries' for the 1997 Union of Reform Judaism publication,

"Where We Stand: Jewish Consciousness on Campus," edited by Allan L. Smith. On behalf of the wonderful organization, Jews for Judaism, I was the weekly guest host for a few years on the Jews for Judaism Chat on America Online. I taught a 12-week course, "Mission Control: How to Respond to the Efforts of Christian Missionaries," at the Houston Jewish Community Center, and also led weekend seminars and two-hour classes on the same subject. I also created a live radio call-in/talk-show in 1997 called "A Show of Faith", co-hosted by a Southern Baptist Minister and a Roman Catholic Priest. The program currently airs weekly on Houston's 1070 KNTH, Sunday nights 7 to 9 p.m., central time. It can also be heard via internet at 1070KNTH.com. Our program website can be found at AShowofFaith.org.

My conversation with the woman at the bookstore, and like-conversations through the years, led me to write this book; however, there are many other reasons that make this book important and useful.

At present, the greatest friends of Israel in the United States appear to be the Evangelical Christian community. If "politics make for strange bedfellows," even members of the Jewish community, in order to ingratiate themselves to the new political bedfellows they have found in Evangelical Christians, choose to ignore the differences between Judaism and Christianity and emphasize our shallow similarities.

With the rise of the Christian missionary groups calling themselves Messianic "Jews," and the successes of the Jews for Jesus organization, the lines between Judaism and Christianity are becoming less and less distinct. This loss of distinction is used to make it easier to convert Jews to Christianity, for if they are not so different after all, then why should it matter if one is a believer in one faith and not the other?

Orthodox rabbis are writing books calling Jesus a rabbi, while other rabbis appear in the media showing a complete lack of understanding of what Christianity believes and what is found in the pages of Christianity's' New Testament, and how this contrasts sharply with the Bible and the beliefs of Judaism.

There is more and more talk about the "Judeo-Christian Tradition," even by Jews who do not understand that, from the Christian perspective, the Jewish aspect of it refers only to that part of Judaism which led up to Christianity. It does not include Rabbinic Judaism that has defined Judaism for virtually the last 2,000-plus years, and which informs every branch of Judaism today. One must also wonder why the Jewish aspect is Latinized into "Judeo," but the Christian aspect remains, simply, "Christian."

In many churches today, Jewish rituals are utilized in the service of Christian celebrations. Many churches, be they Evangelical or Liberal, are holding Passover Seders and celebrating Sukkot, the Festival of Tabernacles. There are Ketubahs, Jewish marriage contracts, being used in Christian marriage services. There are Christian children who are having "Bar Mitzvah" celebrations. All of this blurs the lines between Judaism and Christianity.

More and more people believe that the only difference between Judaism and Christianity is that the latter faith accepts Jesus as the Messiah, while the former does not. They do not know why Jews have continued to reject Jesus as the Messiah, as a savior, and as the son of God. Many Jews, whose knowledge of Judaism is shallow at best, can only say that we Jews do not believe in Jesus because he fulfilled none of the requirements to be the Messiah. Unfortunately, the only requirement they know is that the Messiah will bring peace. They do not realize that there is a whole theology that one must accept first, to believe in Jesus as the Christian Messiah. They do not know that, from Judaism's perspective, this Christian theological foundation is unbiblical and diametrically opposed to what the Bible states.

If one believes that the Bible holds truth within its verses and since Judaism better reflects the theology and beliefs found in the Bible, then Judaism is superior to Christianity in the sense that it holds more of that Biblical Truth. Neither Christians, nor even Jews, are used to hearing any Jew saying that Judaism is a superior faith to Christianity. However, the Jews hear the opposite, subtly or blatantly from Christians, that Christianity is superior to Judaism.

Many Jews, especially those who have been the target of Christian proselytizing, have heard the insult to our faith, that to become a Christian is to become a "completed Jew." Many Jews, if they know nothing else of Christianity, know that to the Conservative Christian, those who reject Jesus as their personal savior, are damned to hell. Many Christians may seem to have learned not to say aloud that their New Testament replaces the "Old Testament" (which is why they call theirs the "New Testament"; see below). They may hesitate or dodge the subject when asked directly if they feel Jews are damned to hell, but the Christian missionary movement continues to believe this. Judaism has never believed that only Jews go to heaven. "The righteous of every nation has a share in the World to Come," it states in the Tosefta to Sanhedrin 13:2. This distinction between the two faiths is also neglected by many Christians.

Jews have been trained since birth to keep a low profile; to be Jewish Uncle Toms. What do I mean by a "Jewish Uncle Tom?" I mean a Jew who is afraid to be outwardly, openly, proudly Jewish. A Jewish Uncle Tom is a Jew who, for example, converses at a normal tone in public, but when the subject shifts to a Jewish topic this person lowers his or her voice. It is a Jew who very willingly wears to Jewish gatherings a Chai or a Star of David on a necklace, or a T-shirt with something Jewish on the front, but who would never think of wearing the Jewish jewelry or a Jewish T-shirt when entering a public place where the majority of others may not be Jewish. I have been with those who will stuff their Jewish jewelry inside their shirts as we entered a mall.

The back of my car has Jewish bumper stickers and a Star of David. I get more negative comments from Jews who are aghast that I so boldly proclaim that the driver of my car is Jewish. They ask me, "Aren't you afraid that a Christian will shoot at you?" These are only a few examples. Jews are simply trained to keep their mouths shut, to not rock any boats, even if it means not rocking the very same boats that were sent to destroy us through conversion, or through the blurring of the lines that distinguish Judaism from Christianity. We are taught to be passive, almost invisible, especially when it comes to emphasizing our differences from the majority around us, a common malady of members of a minority. As the lines between Judaism and Christianity are more and more blurred, this Uncle Tomism may become suicidal.

Furthermore and unfortunately, many Jews have been raised to believe that our faith is just as good as any other faith. We are told self-defeating things, like "every faith has its own room in the mansion of God," or, "there are many paths that all lead to the same God," or that "we all worship the same God." There is only one God. However, if another faith worships someone as God who was not and is not God, then they are committing idolatry. Traditionally, Judaism has believed that only Jews are required to worship the One, True God, and therefore it is not idolatry for Christians or other faiths to worship false gods, but this does not change the fact that the god they worship is not God, and is therefore idolatrous. It is just that, for non-Jews, it is not a sin. They are not committing the sin of idolatry, but what they do worship is, in fact, idolatrous.

If our faith is only as good as the others, if our faith is only as reasonable, only as beneficial, if our faith is not more right than the others, then why would any Jew want to be so different, a part of so very small a minority? Why not just convert to another faith, if, indeed, Judaism is only just as good as and not better than another faith? If we don't believe our faith is better than all other faiths; if we don't believe our faith is more right than all other faiths; if we don't believe our faith is truer than all others then why bother struggling so hard to remain different? Why not just join the majority around us if our faith is only just as good as and not better than all others? This attitude also contributes to the assimilation and eventual loss of Jews to Christianity.

On many levels, the mere idea of saying "I am a Jew" is a way of saying "I choose not to be of another faith." The simple act of choosing to be a Jew, to remain a Jew when both assimilation and conversion out of Judaism are so easy, is to make a statement that the Jewish faith is correct and that all other faiths are incorrect, at least insofar as they disagree with Judaism and the Bible.

We cannot have it both ways. Either Jesus was the Messiah or he was not. Either one human can die for the sins of another or one person cannot die for the sins of another. Either God wants and allows human sacrifice or God does not want or allow human sacrifice. Either a human being is born into the world tainted with original sin, or a human being is not born into the world tainted with original sin. Judaism and Christianity believe in different, mutually exclusive ideas. They cannot both be right because they are in strong disagreement with and in opposition to one another. Either we are right and they are wrong, or they are right and we are wrong. If we are the same, if one faith is just as good as, just as right as, just as beneficial as another faith, then there is no reason to be different and to have suffered as we Jews have suffered simply because we are so different.

This book was also written to help Jews respond to the efforts of Christian missionaries. Only by understanding where Judaism and Christianity disagree and why, can a Jew make the choice to not become a Christian (or can a Gentile make the choice to become a Jew). Not everyone will choose to respond to Christian missionaries with the knowledge they have learned in these pages. Just because one has the knowledge to contrast Judaism with Christianity and show Judaism to be more in keeping with Biblical beliefs, does not mean one must always use this knowledge and point this out to others. You have to choose the battles that are, in your opinion, worth fighting, and how you choose to respond in one circumstance, may not be how you choose to respond in other circumstances or even in the same circumstances at a different time.

For the Jewish community, the idea of responding to the efforts of Christian missionaries presents a great problem. Let us say that I am standing between two Christians. The first is a missionary Christian, one who believes that I am going to hell because I do not believe as he does, and who therefore attempts to convert me to his faith. The second person is a liberal Christian, one who does not believe that I am going to hell, and who does not even consider trying to convert me to his faith. Let us say that, in response to a missionary statement made by the missionary Christian, I make the very simple, most basic statement of disagreement with the missionary Christian that Jesus was not the Messiah.

By doing this, I have not only denied the faith of the missionary Christian, but I have also denied the faith of the liberal Christian. This means that it is virtually impossible to respond to a missionary without the possibility of also insulting the faith of all Christians everywhere, including those who are our friends. This is a problem for Jews, because we have been trained from birth not to hurt another's feelings, especially those who are our friends and would never consider attacking our beliefs.

Will Jews lie on the altar of interfaith dialogue and political correctness, the souls lost to the Jewish community from both conversions through the efforts of Christian missionaries and through the blurring of the lines that separate us?

Responding to Christian missionaries presents a further problem to those who welcome the help of devout Christians in support of the State of Israel. It is a conflict of interest. In their response to missionizing efforts, how can a Jew deny the faith of the very same Christians whose faith leads them to support the State of Israel? The reason this becomes a conflict of interest to the Jews is that those who support the State of Israel from a Christian perspective, are also those most inclined to hope and work for the conversion of the Jews and to blur the lines between the two faiths. They see Christianity as the natural heir to and goal of Judaism.

For some of these Christians, the help they give to the State of Israel is the bait in the net they cast as fishers of men, to be welcomed into Jewish communities, so that they can eventually proselytize their Jewish targets to Christianity.

There is a Christian missionary technique called Bridge Strategy Evangelism. It is also called Friend Strategy Evangelism or Friendship Evangelism as well as other names. The way this Christian missionary technique works is to first determine the perceived needs of the target community. The Christian missionaries will then provide those needs to the target community endearing them to their targets so that one can eventually missionize them. Until they actually begin their attempts at converting their targets to Christianity, they will use the friendship developed with some members of the target group to obtain credibility with other individual targets or to further other goals. The reason why missionizing the initial target group is not immediately engaged, is that one has to develop a reliance on the part of the target group on those missionaries who meet their needs, to further enhance their willingness to listen to the Christian message. This can take years and years to develop.

For the past 50 years, the Jewish community's most often attended events are those which memorialize the Holocaust or that show interest in and support for the State of Israel. When a rabbi wants to get a huge crowd to the synagogue, all that rabbi has to do is a program on Israel or the Holocaust and a huge crowd will attend. But when a rabbi does a program on Judaism, on God, on Torah, then the numbers of those who attend are miniscule at best in comparison.

The needs of the Jewish community, as understood by Evangelical Christians from our own behavior, are to memorialize the Holocaust and to support the State of Israel. When Christians memorialize the Holocaust and support Israel, then I cannot help but wonder if an ulterior motive of theirs is this Bridge Strategy Evangelism. These Evangelical Christians endear themselves to the naive Jewish community; they make the Jewish community reliant on them to fulfill our 'needs' of remembering the Holocaust and supporting the State of Israel. This comes at a price.

Here is just one example. In 2006, members of the Jewish community were objecting to now Supreme Court Justice Alito's appointment, and they made statements against his Conservative political attitudes. Members of the Christian Right began to threaten withdrawal of support for the State of Israel, if the Jewish community did not silence these objections, and stop fighting the Christian Right on such Conservative issues. Effectively they were blackmailing the Jewish community.

I have seen quite often that for the sake of some gain (money in the form of contributions to our Jewish organizations, the feelings of friendship, the feeling that we no longer have to fear Christians because they keep apologizing for the Holocaust, the support for Israel), we are ignoring or setting aside our values. We become afraid to distinguish between Christian values and Jewish values. Ignoring or setting aside one's values for the sake of some gain is the classic definition of prostitution. I have seen Jewish communities ignore the association of Evangelical Christians with Messianic "Jewish" organizations, or with those who pervert our Holidays, our Holy Days, our life cycle events, and our rituals by investing in them Christian meanings as I discuss in this book, because these same Evangelical Christians make a great show of supporting Israel and of memorializing the Holocaust.

There is a price we are paying, and there will be an even greater price to be paid, the more we become reliant on them to meet these supposed needs.

Down the road, when the time is right, they will use the fact that they have been fulfilling our needs and thereby ingratiating themselves to us, as a means to evangelize us. When the vast majority of Jews, again, reject Christianity, just as Jews have so often rejected the Christian message before, anti-Semitism will skyrocket, because their technique won't work to the extent they are hoping. Although I fear the Christian backlash, I do hope that their failure to successfully convert Jews to Christianity will be a result, in some small way, of this book.

We have a choice. We can remain silent, and see more and more members of our Jewish community convert out of Judaism to a faith that denies the most basic Biblical premises of our faith, or we can open our mouths and clarify the contrasts that do, indeed, exist between Judaism and Christianity.

Learning how Judaism and Christianity contrast with each other can be beneficial in numerous ways to the Jewish community. It is beneficial first by strengthening Jews in their own beliefs. It also works to stop the missionaries. They will leave the knowledgeable Jew for the less knowledgeable, no differently than a thief will break into a car that has no defenses rather than one with an obvious burglar alarm. I have often seen how responding to Christian missionary efforts stop or at least slow down the missionaries in their zeal to convert us. More than once, I have seen it result in their conversion from Christianity to Judaism. Not everyone will choose to respond to Christian missionaries the way I teach others to respond. But as the Talmud teaches us, "da mah l'ha-sheev," we should "know how to respond," even if, under some circumstances, we choose not to respond and just walk away.

Learning how Judaism and Christianity contrast with each other can also be beneficial in numerous ways to the Christian community. They can come to understand the Biblical basis of why the Jews, for over 2,000 years, have rejected the Christian message and its theology. Perhaps this will help them accept the fact that knowledgeable Jews, because of their faith in God and in the Bible, will always reject Christianity and Jesus. For some Christians, understanding this might lead them to stop trying to convert us and to respect the Judaism that makes us Jews. Learning how Judaism contrasts with Christianity can lead Christians to a truer understanding of the Jewish community than what is derived from interfaith conversations in which the only thing that is discussed are where the two faiths agree.

I hope and pray that this book will lead those looking for a faith that expresses the truth of the Bible to find it in Judaism. I hope and pray that this book will help sharpen the eternal distinctions between Judaism and Christianity.

May this be God's will!

ACKNOWLEDGEMENTS

Thank you, God, for giving me life, sustaining me, and for allowing me to reach this wonderful time!

Thank you, Marcy Powers for your love and for your support and your encouragement in getting this book written. Thank you, Libbi Federow and Peri Federow for your love and support and encouragement as well.

Thank you, Marcy Powers, Libbi Federow, and Josh White, for your initial editing and critiquing of this book. Thank you, Ted Powers, for editing the first manuscript, and to Cathy Leonard and Rabbi Paul Caplan for editing the final manuscript.

Thank you to all my teachers at Brown University, especially to Jacob Neusner, and all my teachers at the Jerusalem and Cincinnati campuses of the Hebrew Union College-Jewish Institute of Religion, especially Michael Cook, Jonathan Sarna, and Edward Goldman.

Thank you to all those who helped in the creation, maintenance, and improvements of the website, WhatJewsBelieve.org, truly the precursor to this book: Quentelle Barton, Amy Scheinerman, Ed Scheinerman, and Jonah Scheinerman, as well as Wendy Morrison for the most recent update. Thank you Jonas Vilander for turning the website into a smartphone app.

Thank you to the members of Congregation Shaar Hashalom, Houston, Texas, for all of your love and support, especially to the 10th grade Confirmation Classes over the years, in which we would discuss the issues raised in this book.

Thank you, Ron Zaguli, for taking my photograph which appears on the back cover of this book.

We are taught by our tradition that even if a person teaches you only a single letter of the aleph-bet, that you are indebted to that person forever. So am I indebted to all those I have named above, and all those I have not named above, but who have taught me so much over my life, beginning with my parents, Harry and Annette Federow, z'l.

Anything good in these pages belongs to all of you. Only the errors in it are mine.

INTRODUCTION

The beliefs of Judaism and Christianity are diametrically opposed to each other and Jews and Christians disagree on the most fundamental beliefs of their respective faiths. The theologies of the two faiths are mutually exclusive. This book contrasts the most basic fundamental beliefs of these two faiths.

This book will not be easy to read. It will go against the grain of most who read it, who are offended by judgmental statements, who wish to believe in moral equivalency (that there is no objective right or wrong), and who believe there are no objective truths. Those who do not hold the values that distinguish Judaism from other faiths, those who do not view the Bible as authoritative (whether or not they believe God to be its author), will dismiss this book as foolish. Those who remain devoted to their Christian faith might misunderstand the reasons for this book, even though they are discussed at length in the Preface. This book concerns Judaism and how it contrasts with the beliefs of Christianity, and it is difficult to do so without undermining the basic beliefs of Christianity.

Christians may view this as insulting. My intention is not to be insulting, but to defend my faith and my people to those who would try to convert us, to those who would blur the lines that separate Judaism and Christianity, some of whom do so out of fear of losing Christian support for the State of Israel. I will always try to teach Jews, and interested Christians, what we Jews believe and why, how this contrasts with Christian beliefs, and how the Jewish beliefs are more in consonance with Biblical beliefs.

On the other hand, those who are looking for a simple, straightforward explanation of how Judaism and Christianity disagree with one another will welcome what they read. Those Jews who wish to champion Judaism over Christianity will relish it.

The book is divided into two parts. Part I examines what Jews believe and why, in contrast with Christianity. Part II contrasts the way in which the two faiths interpret the same verses in the Hebrew Scriptures. I took the ten verses or sections from the Hebrew Scriptures most often used to proselytize Jews to Christianity and I have given one of the Jewish responses.

I use only verses from the Hebrew Scriptures and verses from the Christian's New Testament to contrast the two faiths. The Christian community is not always impressed by rabbinic quotations. They feel that the true word of God is to be found only in the Bible, and that rabbinic Judaism is merely a man-made faith. This however does not prevent them from misquoting, mistranslating, and misrepresenting statements of the rabbis, just as they do to verses in the Hebrew Scriptures. If it can be used to make it appear that the rabbis reflected Christian theology to further their missionary goals, they use it. Nevertheless, quotations from the Bible are effective in countering their missionary techniques, while those from the rabbis are not. I do, however, quote the rabbis in terms of Jewish law, for the same reason that one cannot only quote the Constitution and its authors regarding American law. Just as American civil law has developed far beyond the days of the American Revolution, so has Jewish law developed far beyond the days of the Bible, and for the same reasons as explained in the fifth chapter in this book regarding Jewish Law.

Some people refer to the Bible as the "Old Testament." No self-respecting Jew should ever refer to our own Bible as the "Old Testament," nor should they allow another to do so in a Jewish context, like our own synagogues or at Jewish gatherings. We Jews do not believe in a "New Testament," so there is no reason to call our Bible the "Old Testament." The term "testament," means "covenant" or "contract." By calling our Bible an "old testament," meaning the "old covenant," Christians imply that their New Testament, their new covenant, has replaced our "old testament." In the Christians' New Testament, misunderstanding Jeremiah 31:31 (which is further explained in Section II of this book), Paul writes,

Hebrews 8:13 *In that he saith, "A new covenant,"*
he hath made the first old. Now that which decayeth and
waxeth old is ready to vanish away.

Our covenant with God is eternal, it will never be replaced, and
it will never vanish away. As Jews sing in the synagogues every week
on the Sabbath, the "v'sham-ru," the Sabbath is an eternal sign of
our eternal covenant with the eternal God.

Exodus 31:16-17 *Wherefore the children of Israel*
shall keep the Sabbath, to observe the Sabbath throughout
their generations, for a perpetual covenant. 17 It is a sign
between me and the children of Israel for ever: for in six days
the Eternal made heaven and earth, and on the seventh day
He rested, and was refreshed.

For a Jew, then, to refer to his or her own Bible as the "Old
Testament," is to deny the eternal nature of God's covenant with
the Jews. Jews should refer to their own Bible as the "Hebrew
Scriptures," or as "The Bible," as I have done in this book, or as the
TaNaCH. (The word, TaNaCH refers to the Hebrew Scriptures.
It is an acronym composed of Torah, the Five Books of Moses;
Nevi'im, the Prophets; and K'tuvim, the Writings, which are the
other Biblical books.)

The Biblical translation I have used for this book is the King
James Version with all of its characteristics both good and bad.
The only thing I changed in the translation was to use "Eternal"
for "Lord." This is because to Christians, the use of the word
"Lord" seems to automatically imply Jesus, since they think that
"Jesus is Lord." Furthermore, the use of the word, "Eternal," is
closer to the meaning of the four-lettered name for God, called the
"tetragrammaton," which is spelled with the equivalent Hebrew
letters for Y, and H, and V, and H. It is derived from the verb, "to
be," and so the "Eternal" is a more accurate translation of this name
for God.

I hope that anyone looking for an explanation of what Jews believe and why, those trying to understand how Judaism and Christianity contrast with each other, those who might be looking into Judaism to possibly convert, and students and teachers of religion, will all benefit from this book.

PART I

A CONTRAST OF BELIEFS

CHAPTER 1

MONOTHEISM AND TRINITY

Jews believe that God is one and indivisible. Jews do not believe in a Trinity.

There are various manifestations of God in the Bible, however this does not mean that each is to be regarded as an entity separate from and unequal to the others, but that they are somehow one and the same. Jews believe that each manifestation of God is only how God chose to be experienced by human beings. We worship God, and not the manifestations of God. We do not feel we have to go through one manifestation of God to commune with a different manifestation of God. When we pray, we pray simply to God, directly to God.

The Hebrew Scriptures tell us that God is one. Deuteronomy 6:4 says the following:

> *Hear, O Israel: The Eternal is our God, The Eternal is one.*

How do we know that the term "one" at the end of the above verse does not refer to some sort of compound unity, meaning that God is made up of different parts that total up to one? The reason we know this is that the word "one" is an adjective. Here, it describes a proper noun, which is the Tetragrammaton, the four-lettered name for God, here translated as "The Eternal." Most people do not realize that this word, translated here as "The Eternal," is actually a name for God, told to us in Exodus 3:14-15. This is because most Bibles translate the Hebrew into "the Lord," which is a title, but the word is a name, the holiest name, of God.

When the word, "one" modifies a person's name, it must mean the person is only one—not a compound one, but rather an absolute one. Let me explain.

Christians may try to explain this by saying that a man named William Jones is "Dad" to his kids, but "Honey" to his wife, "Bill" to his friends, and "Mr. Jones" to his employees. However, in all instances, William Jones has the same knowledge, the same power, and the same will. He is still only one person even though Bill is treated differently and even called by a different name depending on who is speaking to him. However, the Christian New Testament describes Jesus the son as having different knowledge than the Father, a different will than the Father, and different strength than the Father.

In the Christian New Testament, Jesus at one point claims to have different knowledge than other parts of the Christian Trinity. For example, in Matthew 24:36 Jesus says:

> But of that day and hour knoweth no man, no, not the angels of heaven, but my Father only.

Mark 13:32 says the same thing:

> But of that day and hour knoweth no man, no, not the angels which are in heaven, neither the Son, but the Father.

Jesus does not have the same power as other parts of the Christian Trinity. For example, Luke 23:34 says:

> Then said Jesus, Father, forgive them; for they know not what they do. And they parted his raiment, and cast lots.

Why couldn't Jesus himself pardon? If Jesus was the same as the Father, why does he call upon his Father to pardon? Because he was not God, or a part of God (which Christians call a "person" of God), and he therefore did not have the power to forgive, and he knew it.

In Matthew 26:42, Jesus' will is not the same as the will of the Father:

> He went away again the second time, and prayed, saying, O my Father, if this cup may not pass away from me, except I drink it, thy will be done.

This is also found in Mark 14:36:

> And he said, Abba, Father, all things are possible unto thee; take away this cup from me: nevertheless not what I will, but what thou wilt.

In the above statements, Jesus contrasts himself with the Father, with God, because Jesus knew that Jesus was not God.

Indeed, Jesus often contrasts himself with the Father. He does so in John 14:28:

> Ye have heard how I said unto you, I go away, and come again unto you. If ye loved me, ye would rejoice, because I said, I go unto the Father: for my Father is greater than I.

Luke 18:19 provides a similar example:

> And Jesus said unto him, Why callest thou me good? None is good, save one that is, God.

Furthermore, Jesus supposedly said the punishment for speaking against one part of the Trinity is not the same punishment as for speaking against another part of the Trinity. If this is true, then they cannot be the same or the punishments would be the same for speaking against either:

> Matthew 12:32 *And whoever says a word against the Son of man will be forgiven; but whoever speaks against the Holy Spirit will not be forgiven, either in this age or in the age to come.*

If the different parts of the Christian Trinity are not one and the same, if Jesus did not know things that the Father knew, if Jesus did not have the same will as the Father, or the same strength as the Father, then they are separate and unequal to each other. The Christian concept of a Trinity is not monotheism.

There is another issue regarding God's appearances in the Bible. There are more than just three manifestations of God in the Hebrew Scriptures. There is of course, the Spirit of God, as is mentioned in Genesis 1:2:

> *And The Spirit of God (Ruach Elohim) moved over the face of the waters*

But there is also an Evil Spirit of God, as we read in I Samuel 16:23:

> *And it came to pass, when The Evil Spirit of God (Ruach Elohim Raah) was upon Saul, that David took a harp, and played with his hand: so Saul was refreshed, and was well, and the evil spirit departed from him.*

There is also a Lying Spirit of God in I Kings 22:23:

> *Now therefore, behold, the Eternal hath put a lying spirit (Ruach Sheker) in the mouth of all these, thy prophets, and the Eternal hath spoken evil concerning thee.*

In Exodus 12:23, we are told that God will smite the Egyptians. Later in the same verse, however, we see that it is the Destroyer who smites the Egyptians:

For the Eternal will pass through to smite the Egyptians;
and when He seeth the blood upon the lintel, and on the two
side posts, the Eternal will pass over the door, and will not
suffer the Destroyer to come in unto your houses to smite you.

If each manifestation of God is a different entity, then the Destroyer should be seen as a person in God, just as Jesus and the Holy Spirit, the Spirit of God, are seen as persons in God. To this we could add that the Lying Spirit of God should be seen as a person in God, and the Evil Spirit of God should be seen as a person in God. This would mean that, instead of having a Christian Trinity in "the Father, the Son, and the Holy Spirit," Christians should have the Father, the Son, the Holy Spirit, the Lying Spirit, the Evil Spirit, and the Destroyer. This does not even include the Burning Bush, or the pillar of fire by night and the pillar of cloud by day that accompanied the Hebrews when they left slavery in Egypt, according to Exodus 13:21-22.

Why did the Christian community stop at the three persons of the Trinity, when they could have had more persons in the supposed compound unity of God? The reason is that the highest deities in other religions also came in threes.

Babylon had:	[1] Anu	[2] Bel	[3] Ena
India had:	[1] Brahma	[2] Vishnu	[3] Shiva
Ancient Rome had:	[1] Jupiter	[2] Pluto	[3] Neptune
Ancient Greece had:	[1] Zeus	[2] Hades	[3] Poseidon

And so the Christian community took its own Trinity, made up of only the Father, the Son and the Holy Spirit, while disregarding the Lying Spirit, the Evil Spirit, and the Destroyer and other manifestations in the Bible of God.

Jews are taught that God is one, that God is indivisible. This teaching is found throughout the Hebrew Scriptures. In Isaiah 44:6 God tells us:

> *I am the first, and I am the last; and beside me there*
> *is no God.*

When Isaiah tells us God said, "I am the first," this means God has no father. When Isaiah tells us God said, "I am the last," this means God has no literal son. When Isaiah tells us God said, "Besides me there is no God," this means God does not share being God with any other god, or demigod, or semi-god, or "persons" of God.

This is why God tells us in the Ten Commandments, in Exodus 20:3:

> *Thou shalt have no other gods before me.*

Even if you think there are other gods, you cannot have them before the one God. You do not pray to them to get to God, and you do not pray in their names. To do so would be to put them "before God." For example to some, wealth is treated as if it were a god. Here in Exodus we are taught not to hold even those things we treat as if they were a god, before God. God must come first.

Christian missionaries may tell us in speaking of Jesus, "Behold Your God," but the last time we heard something similar, it was in Exodus 32:4, when the ex-slaves pointed to the Golden Calf and said, "These are your gods (Eilay elohecha)."

The Jewish view of God contrasts with the Christian view of God, and the two views cannot denote the same God. For this reason, Christianity's concept of God—one that can be divided into separate and unequal parts to each other, would not be considered monotheism.

CHAPTER 2

GOD IS NOT A MAN

Jews believe that God is God and that humans are humans. We further believe that God does not become human and humans do not become God. Throughout the Hebrew Scriptures, there is a sharp contrast made between God on one hand, and human beings on the other. For instance, there is a reprimand against any human being who claims to be God, or Divine, as we read in Ezekiel 28:2. Here God sends Ezekiel to rebuke the prince of Tyrus for believing that he was God:

> Son of man, say unto the prince of Tyrus, Thus saith the Eternal God; Because thine heart is lifted up, and thou hast said, I am a god, I sit in the seat of God, in the midst of the seas; yet thou art a man, and not God, though thou set thine heart as the heart of God:

Hosea 11:9 tells us that God is not a human being:

> I will not execute the fierceness of mine anger, I will not return to destroy Ephraim: for I am God and not a man; the Holy One in the midst of thee: and I will not enter into the city.

In Numbers and I Samuel there are verses where God specifically tells us that if God were a human being, then he would be a liar, as all human beings do lie on occasion. These verses tell us that if God were a human being, he would be in need of repentance because all human beings sin at some point in their lives. Finally, these verses tell us that if God were a human being, then he would make promises, but not keep them:

> Numbers 23:19 *God is not a man, that he should lie; neither the Son of Man, that he should repent: hath he said, and shall he not do it? Or hath he spoken, and shall he not make it good?*

> 1 Samuel 15:29 And *also the Strength of Israel will not lie nor repent: for he is not a man, that he should repent.*

These verses make it clear that God is not a human being. God does not lie, God does not sin, and God does not break promises like humans do, and like God would do if God were to become a human. God is God and human beings are human beings. God does not become a human being and human beings do not become God.

There are three Jewish Holy Days that celebrate this very idea. They are Passover, Chanukah, and Purim.

Passover

Passover is the celebration of the Exodus of the Jews from slavery in Egypt. God brought the Jews out of slavery by performing miracles, which came in the form of plagues. These plagues were not just against Pharaoh and the Egyptians, as most people think, but against the gods of the Egyptians as well.

> Exodus 12:12 *For I will pass through the land of Egypt this night, and will smite all the firstborn in the land of Egypt, both man and beast; and against all the gods of Egypt I will execute judgment: I am the Eternal.*

For example, Egyptians worshipped the Nile (deified as the Egyptian god Hapi), but Moses, on behalf of God, struck the Nile and it bled. The Egyptians also worshipped the sun, Ra. But one of God's plagues was darkness for three days. The plagues of locusts and hail that destroyed the crops were against the Egyptian gods of the harvest. Finally, the last plague was against the firstborn sons who became the priests of these Egyptian gods. Because Pharaoh was held to be a god by the Egyptians, the text of Exodus 11:5 tells us that the plague of the death of the firstborn went all the way to the throne of Pharaoh:

> And all the firstborn in the land of Egypt shall die,
> from the firstborn of Pharaoh that sitteth upon his throne,
> even unto the firstborn of the maidservant that is behind
> the mill; and all the firstborn of beasts.

The holiday of Passover has a way of saying, "Sorry, Pharaoh, you are not God!"

Chanukah

Antiochus of Syria wanted to unify his empire by making all of its inhabitants into Hellenists—followers of Zeus. But the Jews refused, of course, because they believed, and still believe, in only one God. Antiochus saw this as insurrection and began persecuting the Jews. Antiochus called himself Antiochus Epiphanes, which means, "Antiochus who is god manifested." The Jews eventually rebelled, giving us Chanukah.

The holiday of Chanukah has a way of saying, "Sorry, Antiochus, you are not God!"

Purim

Purim is the holiday that celebrates the events of the Biblical book of Esther. In this story there is a character named Haman who hated the Jews because the Jewish hero Mordechai would not bow down to him, (see Esther 3:2-4). Queen Esther intervened on behalf of her people, which led to the death of Haman and gave us the holiday of Purim.

The holiday of Purim has a way of saying, "Sorry, Haman, you are not God!"

Each of these three holidays celebrates the ideas that God is God, that humans are humans, that God does not become a human, and that humans do not become God.

This means the distinction between God and man is basic to the faith of the Jewish People. Christianity does not make this distinction, a practice that was also common in the ancient pagan world. The simple description, 'his mother was human and his father was God,' sounds like Jesus. However, it is also a description of Hercules, whose human mother was Alcmene and whose father was Zeus. It is a description as well of Dionysus, whose human mother was Semele and whose father was also Zeus. It is a description as well of Perseus whose human mother was Danae and whose father, again, was Zeus. Furthermore, Danae was not made pregnant by Zeus through the sex act, but rather through a shower of gold. This means that Perseus' birth was like that from a virgin.

Judaism's theology is one of absolute monotheism, and one that separates man and God. The confusion of man with the gods is a hallmark of pagan faiths. The theology of Christianity is far closer to the Hellenist and Roman dying/saving man/gods than anything one finds in the Bible or in Judaism.

CHAPTER 3
THE SATAN VERSUS A DEVIL

Jews believe in the existence of The Satan, and not in the existence of the devil. There is a difference between the concept of the Satan and the concept of the devil, even though the words 'Satan' and 'devil' are used interchangeably in Christianity.

For Jews, anything that even remotely conflicts with the idea that God is one and indivisible will be rejected because it precludes true, pure monotheism, as we discussed in Chapter 1. The idea that there is a God in heaven above who fights against a god of the underworld over human souls is not monotheism. Other faiths had this same duality:

Ancient Greece had:	Zeus/Hades
Ancient Rome had:	Jupiter/Pluto
Christianity has:	God/Devil

Now, of course, Judaism and the Bible tell of a character called, "The Satan." Almost every time the term is used in the Hebrew Scriptures, it reads, "HaSaTaN," which means "The Satan." In most translations, however, the definite article is missing.

The concept of The Satan is radically different from the idea of the devil. For Christians, the devil has power and authority in and of himself. However, in the Bible, The Satan only has power granted by God, and has no authority. The Satan is described in only a few places in the Hebrew Scriptures, and in every instance, he is an angel who works *for* God, not against God, and must get permission from God for everything he does. Chronicles, Job,

Psalms, and Zechariah are the only places in the Hebrew Scriptures where The Satan is mentioned. In each instance, the job description of The Satan is to act like a modern district attorney. He accuses and shows evidence against a defendant. Furthermore, like a district attorney, The Satan must obtain permission from God, the Judge, to begin a sting operation.

In the following quotation from the book of Job, take note of who is doing the talking, as The Satan asks God for permission to act against Job:

> Job 2:3-6: *And the Eternal said unto Satan, Hast thou considered my servant Job, that there is none like him in the earth, a perfect and an upright man, one that feareth God, and escheweth evil? And still he holdeth fast his integrity, although thou <The Satan> movest me <God> against him, to destroy him without cause. 4 And Satan answered the Eternal, and said, Skin for skin, yea, all that a man hath will he give for his life. 5 But put forth thine hand <God's hand> now, and touch his bone and his flesh, and he will curse thee to thy face. 6 And the Eternal said unto Satan, Behold, he is in thine hand; but save his life.*

In the above verses, The Satan obtains permission from God to act against Job, which is granted to him in verse 6, above. The Satan has no power or authority of his own, like a district attorney in the American Judicial system; he must obtain permission from the judge in everything he does. So, too, must The Satan.

Furthermore, the Biblical text paints this same picture of The Satan in what appears to be the end of a court scene. In the following two quotations, The Satan stands in opposition to the accused as a district attorney might stand at the end of a television court drama. The first angel of God mentioned below is like a Defense Attorney, while The Satan is his accuser, like the District Attorney or Prosecutor.

Zechariah 3:1-2 *And he showed me Joshua the high priest standing before the angel of the Eternal, and Satan standing at his right hand to accuse him. 2 And the Eternal said unto Satan, "The Eternal rebukes thee, O Satan; even the Eternal that hath chosen Jerusalem rebukes thee: is not this a brand plucked out of the fire?"*

Psalm 109:6-7 *Set thou a wicked man over him, and let Satan stand at his right hand. 7 When he shall be judged, let him be condemned, and let his prayer become sin.*

What is going on in the verses from Zechariah above? Joshua the High Priest appears to be on trial. He was one of the captives taken into the Exile, into Babylonia. It was time to return to Jerusalem to rebuild The Temple. The Satan, as the Accuser, is claiming that Joshua the High Priest has no right to return, since he was one of the guilty who was exiled. However, God, the Judge, is saying that Joshua was like a 'brand plucked out of the fire,' meaning that the exile purified him, and that God was siding with the Defense against The Satan, the Prosecuting Attorney.

There is also a verse in the Bible that shows that it is God, the Creator and Ruler of the whole universe, who is responsible for both good and evil, and not a devil or god of the underworld who is responsible for the evil:

Isaiah 45:5-7 *I am the Eternal, and there is none else, there is no god beside me: I girded thee, though thou hast not known me: 6 That they may know from the rising of the sun, and from the west, that there is none beside me. I am the Eternal, and there is none else. 7 I form the light, and create darkness: I make peace, and create evil: I the Eternal do all these things.*

One sees in many parts of our popular culture, the Christian idea that the devil competes with God over human souls. The phrase that one often hears is that the devil might entice someone to 'sell his soul to the devil.' This is simply unbiblical as well. It is God who owns our souls, and God gives our souls only temporarily to us while we are alive on this earth. We cannot sell what does not belong to us. As we are taught in Ezekiel 18:4:

> *Behold, all souls are mine; as the soul of the father, so also the soul of the son is mine . . .*

And at the end of our lives, our soul returns to God who lent it to us:

> Ecclesiastes 12:7 *Then shall the dust return to the earth as it was: and the spirit shall return unto God who gave it.*

For God, for the Bible, and for Judaism, to have an entity that competes with God, that has power and authority of his own, is to have two gods, and this violates the basic Jewish Biblical idea of monotheism.

Some Christians may claim that the devil is not a God, but is merely a fallen angel, one who tried to overthrow God in heaven, and who was kicked out along with those in heaven who followed him and became his demons.

There is a verse in the Hebrew Scriptures that appears to reflect this concept:

> Isaiah 14:12-14 *How art thou fallen from heaven, O Lucifer, son of the morning! How art thou cut down to the ground, which didst weaken the nations! 13 For thou hast said in thine heart, I will ascend into heaven, I will exalt my throne above the stars of God: I will sit also upon the mount of the congregation, in the sides of the north: 14 I will ascend above the heights of the clouds; I will be like the most High.*

If one were to look at the entire context in which this verse is found, beginning with Isaiah 14:4, one would see that this entire section is devoted to the human King of Babylon, who believed that he was a god:

> Isaiah 14:4 *That thou shalt take up this proverb against the King of Babylon, and say; how hath the oppressor ceased! The golden city ceased!*

The entire passage taunts the King of Babylon for being once so exalted, but who was then brought low. The verse likens him to a falling star. In fact, the verse in this translation uses the name Lucifer, which is Latin for 'light-bearer,' and refers to the planet Venus in the early morning sky, also called 'the morning star.' The verses are saying that as Venus, the morning star, announces the new day but dips below the horizon as the sun rises, so did the King of Babylon rise in the night but fall from his lofty place.

This interpretation of these verses originates not in Judaism, but in ancient pagan religions. According to the religious texts found at Ras Shamra in ancient Syria, Athtar tried to displace the god Baal, but instead he descended from the heavens to become the god of the underworld.

Although some Christians claim that the devil is not a god, this is not how their New Testament portrays him.

First, in the Gospels, Jesus is tempted by the devil in Luke 4:1-13:

> *And Jesus being full of the Holy Ghost returned from Jordan, and was led by the Spirit into the wilderness, 2 Being forty days tempted of the devil. And in those days he did eat nothing: and when they were ended, he afterward hungered. 3 And the devil said unto him, if thou be the Son of God, command this stone that it be made bread. 4 And Jesus answered him, saying, it is written, that man shall not live by bread alone, but by every word of God. 5 And the devil, taking him up into a high mountain, showed unto him all the kingdoms of the world in a moment of time.*

6 And the devil said unto him, All this power will I give thee, and the glory of them: for that is delivered unto me; and to whomsoever I will I give it. 7 If thou therefore wilt worship me, all shall be thine. 8 And Jesus answered and said unto him, Get thee behind me, Satan: for it is written, Thou shalt worship the Lord thy God, and him only shalt thou serve. 9 And he brought him to Jerusalem, and set him on a pinnacle of the temple, and said unto him, If thou be the Son of God, cast thyself down from hence: 10 For it is written, He shall give his angels charge over thee, to keep thee: 11 And in their hands they shall bear thee up, lest at any time thou dash thy foot against a stone. 12 And Jesus answering said unto him, It is said, Thou shalt not tempt the Lord thy God. 13 And when the devil had ended all the temptation, he departed from him for a season.

Here in Luke, as well as in Matthew 4, the devil tempts Jesus. Since Jesus himself quotes Deuteronomy 6:16, *You shall not tempt the Eternal your God*, to the devil, and the devil was trying to tempt Jesus, it implies that the devil did not recognize Jesus as Divine. Furthermore, the verses above say that the devil showed to Jesus all the kingdoms in the world, claiming that it was in his power to give them to another. Only the god of this world would have such power, which is how Paul refers to the devil in 2 Corinthians 4:4:

But if our gospel be hid, it is hid to them that are lost: In whom the god of this world hath blinded the minds of them which believe not, lest the light of the glorious gospel of Christ, who is the image of God, should shine unto them.

The Greek of the verses above from 2 Corinthians uses the term, "theos," for the word "god," in both the phrase, the "god of this world," meaning the devil, as well as in the phrase, "the image of God." And so, for the devil to be "theos," as God is "theos," means that Christianity sees the devil as a god.

Another name for the devil in the Christian's New Testament is "Beelzebub," found in Matthew 12, Mark 3, and Luke 11. This name, which in Hebrew is "baal-zevoov," means "Lord of the Flies." The term "Lord" or "Baal," is used to refer to the devil, just as the term "Lord" is used to refer to Jesus or to God. Furthermore, "Baal" was the name of a god in the ancient pagan world.

The New Testament juxtaposes God, the Ruler of the Heavens, with the devil, the god of this world. This is not monotheism, but polytheism, and God, Judaism, and the Bible reject it as such.

CHAPTER 4

THE NATURE OF HUMANITY

The Christian concept of original sin is that because Adam and Eve sinned in the Garden of Eden, all human beings are born not only with a tendency to sin, but also with the guilt of Adam and Eve. For this guilt, all human beings die, as we read in I Corinthians 15:21-22:

> *For since by man came death, by man came also the resurrection of the dead. 22 For as in Adam all die, even so in Christ shall all be made alive.*

The concept that we die because of the sin of Adam and Eve in the Garden of Eden is simply unbiblical. The Biblical text tells us that Adam and Eve were not removed from the Garden of Eden because they sinned. The first time the Bible uses the term, "sin," it is not in reference to Adam and Eve, but in reference to the jealousy of Cain against Abel in Genesis 4:7. Rather, Adam and Eve were removed from the Garden of Eden because there was another tree in the garden from which God did not want them to eat. That tree was the Tree of Life.

> Genesis 3:22-24 *And the Eternal God said, Behold, the man is become as one of us, to know good and evil: and now, lest he put forth his hand, and take also of the Tree of Life, and eat, and live forever: 23 Therefore the Eternal God sent him forth from the garden of Eden, to till the ground from whence he was taken. 24 So he drove out*

the man; and he placed at the east of the Garden of Eden
Cherubims, and a flaming sword that turned every way, to
keep the way of the Tree of Life.

If, according to Christian theology on original sin, I die because Adam and Eve sinned, it violates the first part of Deuteronomy 24:16:

The fathers shall not be put to death for the children;
neither shall the children be put to death for the fathers.
Every man shall be put to death for his own sin.

One does not die because Adam and Eve sinned. It is against what the Bible says.

Human beings always have a choice. You can choose death or you can choose life, but it is your choice. If you do not have free will, then you cannot be held responsible for your choices because you do not even have a choice. If you are a sinner because you are born that way, it is not your fault that you sin. It is simply the way God made you. In this case, if you sin, I cannot blame you, rather I must blame God. You should not be held responsible for your sins because God made you a sinner; God brought you into the world, knowing that you were going to be a sinner. But if you have free will, if you can choose between doing good and evil, you are now responsible for your own choices and your own behavior.

Anyone with a dog can probably remember calling their pet a "good dog." But is a dog really capable of making a moral choice that leads you to call him good? No. The dog knows only reward and punishment.

If you think about it, the same situation should apply to Adam and Eve. Before eating the fruit of The Tree of the Knowledge, Adam and Eve did not know the difference between good and evil. Because they did not know the difference between good and evil, they did not know that it was evil to disobey God by eating from the tree. Therefore, they are not committing a sin; they are not making a moral choice between good and evil by eating the fruit. As I mentioned before, the word "sin" is not even used in the Bible when referring to Adam and Eve. This is why the Bible never referred to it as a sin.

Genesis also mentions another tree in the Garden of Eden, which was the Tree of Life. If Adam and Eve had to eat the fruit of The Tree of Life to become immortal, then God made them mortal to begin with. Adam and Eve were created in such a way that death was a natural part of their existence, from the moment of their creation.

The full Biblical text of Genesis 3:22-24 tells us that Adam and Eve were almost like God and the Angels, and they were because both God and the Angels knew the difference between good and evil. However, they are immortal as well. Because Adam and Eve ate the fruit of The Tree of the Knowledge of Good and Evil, they, like God and the Angels, knew the difference between Good and Evil. However, Adam and Eve were not yet immortal because they had not yet eaten from the Tree of Life. Had they been able to also eat from the Tree of Life, then they would have completely been like God and Angels, because they would have known the difference between Good and Evil, and they would have also become immortal. Therefore, God separated Adam and Eve from the Tree of Life by forcing them to leave the garden, and then God blocked the way to the Tree of Life with the Cherubims and the flaming sword. This is explicitly what the verses in Genesis 3:22-24 tell us. This means that Adam and Eve did not bring death into the world. We human beings do not die because of their sin; we die because God made death a part of life from the moment of creation:

One can also know that death was created as a natural part of life from God's first commandment in Genesis 1:22 to the animals. This was before Adam and Eve were created, which is in Genesis 1:26. God tells them to be fruitful and to multiply. Why? So they could replace themselves, since they, too, were created mortal.

Remember also, that no one else can die for the sins of others. This will be discussed in Chapter 6. This means that even if one believed that Adam and Eve sinned in the Garden of Eden (which they didn't), their descendants cannot die, and do not die, for the guilt of any sin committed by Adam and Eve.

In general, parents want their children to grow up and leave the house. God, the perfect parent, also wants Adam and Eve to "get out of the house," to be more on their own. How does a child "grow up" and prove his or her independence? They disobey. And by disobeying, a child is forced to take responsibility for his or her behavior and become an adult. Adam and Eve are the kids being forced out of the "house." After eating from the tree, they know the difference between good and evil. They are growing up and are forced out on their own because they have free will. Having the ability to choose between Good and Evil, they are now, like all adults, responsible and culpable for their choices.

This is how the world works. We are born into the world innocent and not knowing the differences between Right and Wrong. But as we grow up, we learn, and make our own decisions, get out on our own, and we become responsible for our own choices. This is how the Bible treats Adam and Eve, and it tells the saga of growing up. We do not suffer for the sin of Adam and Eve. They did not bring death into the world. We die because that is how God made the world from the moment of Creation. To look at Genesis in any other way, is unbiblical.

CHAPTER 5

JEWISH LAW

Before we contrast the Jewish view of Jewish Law with the Christian view of Jewish Law, we must understand what we are talking about when we say, "Jewish Law." At the time of Jesus, there were, first and foremost, the laws of God given to the People of Israel through Moses and found in the Torah.

When the New Testament writers wrote of "the law," they would have mainly been referring to these laws found in the Torah, as well as the rest of the Hebrew Scriptures, which were just then in the process of becoming standardized as the Jewish Biblical canon.

Additionally, Jesus makes references to the earliest laws of the Pharisees, who were the precursors to the rabbis. Besides the laws given by God in the Hebrew Scriptures and the laws that had already been established by the Pharisees, there were no other Jewish laws.

Of all the books in the Christian New Testament, most were written by Paul. Truly, Paul's theology has impacted Christianity more than that of Jesus, as we shall see. There seems to be a difference between Jesus' view of Jewish Law, and Paul's view of those same laws.

Regarding the laws of God as given to the Jews through Moses, Jesus states in Matthew 5:17-20:

> *Think not that I am come to destroy the law, or the prophets: I am not come to destroy, but to fulfill. 18 For verily I say unto you, till heaven and earth pass, one jot or one tittle shall in no wise pass from the law, till all be fulfilled. 19 Whosoever therefore shall break one of these least commandments, and shall teach men so, he shall be called the*

least in the kingdom of heaven: but whosoever shall do and
teach them, the same shall be called great in the kingdom of
heaven. 20 For I say unto you, that except your righteousness
shall exceed the righteousness of the scribes and Pharisees, ye
shall in no case enter into the kingdom of heaven.

In the above verses, Jesus respects Jewish Law, as well as the laws
of the Pharisees, and does not want to change any aspect of either.

Furthermore, Jesus, regarding the laws of the Pharisees (again,
the precursors to the rabbis), stated in Matthew 23:1-3:

Then spoke Jesus to the multitude, and to his disciples, 2
Saying, The scribes and the Pharisees sit in Moses' seat: 3 All
therefore whatsoever they bid you observe, that observe and
do; but do not ye after their works: for they say, and do not.

By saying that the Pharisees, as well as the scribes, "sit in Moses'
seat," Jesus was saying that they hold the same authority as did Moses,
and that they should be obeyed. This means that here, Jesus was saying
that the laws of the Bible as well as the laws of the Pharisees (who
became the rabbis), should be obeyed. Jesus' objection was not against
the laws of the Pharisees, but rather it was against the fact that the
Pharisees themselves did not obey them. Jesus attacked their hypocrisy,
and not their laws, he was directing his followers to obey their laws.

As we shall see, Paul had a very negative view of Jewish Law, and
it is the views of Paul that have been prevalent in Christianity, rather
than Jesus' view of Jewish law. On the other hand, non-Jews were
never commanded by God to follow His Laws. The only people
who were at Mt. Sinai were the Jews, the Hebrews as well as the
Egyptians who left with them and became Jews as a result. Once
Christianity became largely made up of Gentiles, of non-Jews, there
was no reason for them to keep the Biblical laws since the Gentiles
were not given the commandments in the first place.

There are many misconceptions that Christianity holds towards
Jewish law. Not all of these views are derived from Paul. Many of
them might be familiar to the reader.

Some of Christianity's misunderstandings include:

1. That Jewish Laws are only about rituals
2. That Jews added more and more laws to the Bible that are unnecessary and that are not divine.
3. That the purpose of Jewish Law is to condemn those who don't obey them
4. That Jews keep Jewish Law in order to be justified, their guilt removed, so that they can go to heaven
5. That the Jewish Laws are too many for one person to obey, and that no one person can obey every law
6. That to break any one Jewish Law is the same as breaking any other law, and to break one law is to break them all
7. That the observance of or obedience to Jewish Law is an All-or-Nothing proposition
8. That Jewish Laws become obsolete if one person perfectly obeys, or fulfills, those laws
9. That by punishing one person, another person's guilt for sins can be removed.

1. That Jewish Laws are only about rituals

The stereotype is that Jewish laws are all about the minute rituals that one has to do on a daily basis. This is simply wrong. If one were to actually pick up the Bible and read it one would find something very interesting. Jewish laws were created for the same kinds of things that any neighborhood or city or county or state or country would create laws for, and for the same reasons.

If my dog is running across your lawn and falls into a hole in your yard that you had dug for whatever reason, and breaks its leg, what happens? Who is responsible? Is this a law that is ritual in nature? Countering the myth that Jewish laws are only about rituals, this same law is found in the Torah in Exodus 21:33-34:

And if a man shall open a pit, or if a man shall dig a
pit, and not cover it, and an ass or an ox falls therein, 34
The owner of the pit shall make it good, and give money to
the owner of them, and the dead beast shall be his.

If you are going to build a house, there are laws, building codes, that govern how your house must be constructed, and how the safety of those who live in it and near it, are to be insured by its construction. This, too, is found in the Bible in Deuteronomy 22:8:

When thou buildest a new house, then thou shalt make
a battlement for thy roof, that thou bring not blood upon
thine house, if any man fall from thence.

The verse above commands the Jews to build a fence around the roof of a house, so no one will fall off of it, truly a Biblical building code.

Of course there are Jewish laws that regard Jewish rituals. In the United States there are laws that govern how one displays the U.S. flag and how one recites the Pledge of Allegiance, which are also rituals. But understand that Jewish law also governs areas that have nothing to do with ritual. As a matter of fact, most people would characterize these laws as civil, but they remain a part of our Jewish religious laws. Jewish laws, no differently than any other nation's laws, cover the exact same subjects, rituals, torte (lawsuit), liability, building codes, etc. The difference is that for the Jews, these laws and those laws that are derived from the same God-given Biblical values are also considered God-given.

2. **That Jews added more and more laws to the Bible that are unnecessary and that are not divine.**

Where in the U.S. Constitution does it say that one must drive a car at a speed of 20 miles per hour in a school zone? Of course, the U.S. Constitution does not contain any laws that pertain to automobiles.

Automobiles did not exist at the time the U.S. Constitution was written. When the car was invented, new laws in keeping with the values found in the U.S. Constitution had to be created to cover the new situations created by this new invention. That is why not all laws of the United States are to be found in the U.S. Constitution.

This also explains why not all Jewish laws are to be found in the Bible. Judaism also had to come up with new laws, in keeping with the Divine values and ethics of the Bible, for the new inventions and new situations that developed after the Biblical period. This is why there is Rabbinic Law.

American life today is not defined solely by the laws in the U.S. Constitution, but rather also by the laws created by Congress over the last 200-plus years, as well as by various court cases and other precedents. Similarly, Judaism is not just the religion of the Bible, but rather Judaism is also the religion of the rabbinic interpretation of the Bible.

There are verses in the Bible that require interpretation, because the Bible gives no indication regarding how they are supposed to be carried out. Probably the most obvious example is seen from the Biblical law of placing the mezuzah on the door-posts of one's home. All that the text in Deuteronomy 6:9 states is:

> *And thou shalt write them upon the door posts of thy house, and upon thy gates.*

The Bible never tells us what is supposed to be written, nor does it indicate how or where these commandments should be placed on the door posts. In order to be carried out, this verse requires interpretation. This simple example shows the need for the Oral Law, the interpretations of the rabbis.

This is no different than Christianity, which is not the religion of the New Testament, but rather it is the religion of the interpretation of the New Testament, by the leaders of the various churches and denominations over the past 2,000-plus years.

The way in which Christianity baptizes someone, and when they baptize someone, can show how Christianity is the result of the interpretation of the Christians' New Testament rather than the religion of the New Testament. Christians are divided as to what age one is to be baptized, and the way in which one is to be baptized. Roman Catholics will baptize a baby at birth, while most Protestant denominations will only baptize a person when he or she is old enough to understand what it means to be baptized, and who understands what it means to accept Jesus as his or her personal savior. Roman Catholic priests will baptize an infant just by sprinkling water on the baby's forehead, while many Protestant denominations will only baptize by fully immersing the person in water. These differences in how and when one is baptized are a result of the differing interpretations of the New Testament by the various denominations and their leaders.

The Christian New Testament is not clear as to how or when baptism should be done. At one point, in Acts 16:31, Jesus tells a man that if he believes, he and his whole house will be saved:

> *And they said, Believe on the Lord Jesus Christ, and thou shalt be saved, and thy house.*

One could possibly interpret that to mean that the entire household would be ready to be baptized if only the father accepted Christianity, and that could include infant children. This interpretation could justify the baptism of infants, whose parents, or whose parent accepted Jesus:

The Christian New Testament is also unclear as to how one is to be baptized. Baptism as a Christian ritual is derived from the story in Matthew where Jesus himself was baptized:

> Matthew 3:16 *And Jesus, when he was baptized, went up straightway out of the water: and, lo, the heavens were opened unto him, and he saw the Spirit of God descending like a dove, and lighting upon him.*

All the text states is that after Jesus was baptized, he "went up straightway out of the water." It does not say how deep the water was, it could have been only ankle deep. One can say that a man who steps out of a bathtub "came out of the water," but that does not mean that his whole body was completely submerged. A ladle can be dipped in the water, but only the bowl of the ladle is placed in the water, and not the whole ladle. Neither the handle nor the hand holding the handle is ever completely submerged. The text of the New Testament is never clear on how or when someone is to be baptized.

Those Christian denominations that interpret this verse from Matthew 3:16 to mean that Jesus was completely immersed in water will baptize by completely immersing the person in water. Those Christian denominations that interpret this same verse to mean that Jesus was not fully immersed will not demand a full immersion in water for their baptisms.

The way in which the various denominations of Christianity interpreted these verses and incorporated their interpretations into their rituals is no different than the way in which the rabbis interpreted verses from the Hebrew Scriptures and then incorporated these rabbinic interpretations into the Jewish rituals. The Talmud and the Oral Law is made up of the interpretations of the rabbis. Like the Talmud in this regard, the interpretations made by the early Christians of their New Testament verses which were applied to new situations and to solve new problems is their oral tradition.

The Jews did not merely add more and more laws to the already existing Biblical laws. They were faced with new situations and had to apply the Divine Biblical laws with their Divine Biblical values and ethics to those new situations, in order to continue to do the will of God. That is why Jewish laws are considered to be God-given, regardless of whether or not they are found in the Bible, Talmud, or in other Jewish literature.

3. That the purpose of Jewish Law is to condemn those who don't obey them

Paul in the Christian New Testament seems to hold a very negative view of Jewish Law, the laws given by God to the Jewish

People through Moses on Mount Sinai as well as the laws given to the Jewish People afterwards. Paul writes that these laws were given by God to teach the Jews that they were sinners and incapable of keeping these laws, in order to further teach them that they would eventually need the saving death of Jesus on the cross to remove from them their guilt. The purpose of these God-given laws, according to Paul and to Christianity, is to teach us that what we do is wrong, making us sinners, so that we can understand our guilt that only Jesus can remove. Paul writes in Romans 3:19-24:

> *Now we know that what things soever the law saith, it saith to them who are under the law: that every mouth may be stopped, and all the world may become guilty before God.*

Further, Paul writes in Galatians 3:10-13, that the law is a curse, because its function is to teach the people that, since they cannot keep the law, they are cursed by it. Since Jesus came, the law is no longer binding on those who believe in him, and therefore his followers are no longer condemned, or cursed, by the law. All those who accept Jesus are forgiven of their sins, and the law no longer curses them, since, being Christians, they are no longer obligated to keep those laws:

> Galatians 3:10-13 *For as many as are of the works of the law are under the curse: for it is written, Cursed is every one that continueth not in all things which are written in the book of the law to do them. 11 But that no man is justified by the law in the sight of God, it is evident: for, the just shall live by faith. 12 And the law is not of faith: but, The man that doeth them shall live in them. 13 Christ hath redeemed us from the curse of the law, being made a curse for us: for it is written, Cursed is every one that hangeth on a tree.*

Another example can be seen a few verses later, in Galatians 3:23-25, where Paul writes that God's law was like a schoolmaster, teaching those who were given the law, namely the Jews, that they were sinners. However, one's faith in Jesus took away the sins that the inevitable disobedience to the law would bring; meaning that one no longer needed the law, the schoolmaster:

> Galatians 3:23-25 *But before faith came; we were kept under the law, shut up unto the faith which should afterwards be revealed. 24 Wherefore the law was our schoolmaster to bring us unto Christ, that we might be justified by faith. 25 But after that faith is come, we are no longer under a schoolmaster.*

Paul consistently taught that the reason why God gave the law was to make all individuals aware of the fact that they were sinners, since they were not capable of keeping the law perfectly. As a result of learning from the law that they were sinners, people would then understand that they needed Jesus to die for their sins, and remove from them their sinful guilt-ridden state.

First, would God give a law that He knew no one could keep, and then condemn everyone for not keeping that law? Obviously not. Is God so cruel that He would bring a person into existence, give him or her, a law or set of laws that he or she was incapable of obeying, and then condemn him or her to an eternity of torture for not keeping the law that He gave? God is not cruel. If God is all-merciful, if God is compassionate, if God is forgiving and kind, then God would not do such a thing.

What then is the reason for Jewish laws? God, who is merciful and compassionate and forgiving and kind, gave laws to the Jews for the very same reason that loving Parents give their children laws. They knew that the children will have a better life than they would have without any laws. Parents who love the child do not say to the child, "I love you, now go do whatever you want." Loving parents lay down guidelines for their children, and they do so because they love them and want the best for them. A life lived with no discipline, with no guidelines, no laws by which to live will become a life of selfishness and cruelty to others. Furthermore, when a parent gives the child such laws, the parent does not want the child to obey because it pleases the parent, but rather because the laws are for the benefit of the child.

To understand how law works in Judaism, let us use an analogy of driving a car. This analogy of Jewish law to the laws of driving a car can help us understand many aspects of Jewish law.

Would anyone wish to live in a city that has no laws to govern the way in which we drive? Would anyone truly wish to drive in a city that has no traffic laws, no speed laws, no laws of right of way, no laws at all that govern our driving? Truthfully, the laws created by city and state help us drive. They help to make driving a safe experience for those behind the wheel—the passengers, as well as the pedestrians who walk in or near traffic.

If one agreed with the attitude of Paul in the verses cited above regarding Jewish law and applied it to driving, then the reason the laws are given to limit one's speed in a school zone, for example, would be to teach drivers that since they will eventually speed and get a ticket, that they are speeders and lawbreakers. According to Paul, all drivers are in need of forgiveness for breaking the law by driving faster than 20 miles per hour in a school zone even before they get behind the wheel of a car!

Why then is there such a law, limiting one's speed when going through a school zone? Because it is easier and quicker to stop a car going 20 than it is to stop a car going 35. Furthermore, so that, God forbid, if one accidently strikes a student, the student is less likely to be hurt by a car going 20 miles per hour than if the student got hit with a car going at 35. The law of driving a car in a school zone by limiting the speed to 20 miles per hour is given for the sake of the driver and for the sake of the students. One does not obey the law limiting one's speed because it would please the Judge, but rather because it is beneficial to the students and to the driver to obey the law.

So often, Christians will say that Judaism is the religion of law, while Christianity is the religion of love. What they fail to realize is that while it is true that Judaism is a religion of law, these laws were given to us by God out of His love for us. We, in turn, obey the law out of our love for God. This is what is meant by the passage from Deuteronomy 6:4-9, recited by Jews in our religious services:

> *Hear, O Israel: the Eternal is our God, the Eternal is one. 5 And thou shalt love the Eternal thy God with all thine heart, and with all thy soul, and with all thy might. 6 And these words, which I command thee this day, shall be upon thine heart: 7 and thou shalt teach them diligently unto thy children, and shalt talk of them when thou sittest in thine house, and when thou walkest by the way, and when thou liest down, and when thou risest up. 8 And thou shalt bind them for a sign upon thine hand, and they shall be for frontlets between thine eyes. 9 And thou shalt write them upon the door posts of thy house, and upon thy gates.*

These verses connect our love of God with obedience to His commandments, and the obedience to His laws helps us live our lives to the fullest, just like the laws of driving make for a better driving experience. As we read in Leviticus 18:4-5:

> *My judgments shall ye do, and my statutes shall ye keep, to walk therein: I am the Eternal your God. 5 Ye shall therefore keep my statutes, and my judgments: which if a man do, he shall live in them: I am the Eternal.*

4. That Jews keep Jewish Law in order to be justified, their guilt removed, in order to go to heaven

In the Christian New Testament, Paul often makes a comparison between one's faith and one's works or deeds. To Paul, it is the faith in Jesus as one's personal savior that removes the guilt of sin and enables one to get to heaven. Since salvation from eternal damnation is Paul's main concern, he believes that salvation is a main concern of Judaism. Because he sees faith as the means to salvation from eternal damnation, and since Judaism is a religion of law, he states that in Judaism, the obedience to Jewish law is our means to salvation. He is completely wrong on all counts:

Romans 3:20-24 *Therefore by the deeds of the law there shall no flesh be justified in his sight: for by the law is the knowledge of sin. 21 But now the righteousness of God without the law is manifested, being witnessed by the law and the prophets; 22 Even the righteousness of God which is by faith of Jesus Christ unto all and upon all them that believe: for there is no difference: 23 For all have sinned, and come short of the glory of God; 24 Being justified freely by his grace through the redemption that is in Christ Jesus.*

Romans 3:28 *Therefore we conclude that a man is justified by faith without the deeds of the law.*

Galatians 2:16 *Knowing that a man is not justified by the works of the law, but by the faith of Jesus Christ, even we have believed in Jesus Christ, that we might be justified by the faith of Christ, and not by the works of the law: for by the works of the law shall no flesh be justified.*

These verses indicate a fundamental misunderstanding of Jewish law. Repeatedly, Paul writes that the law cannot 'justify' those who follow them. To be "justified" means to be forgiven for our sins, to be made righteous or without the guilt of sin, which then enabled the person to go to heaven. Paul believed that the Jews keep Jewish law in order to be forgiven for our sins, enabling us to go to heaven. Paul believed that only one's faith in Jesus would enable them to go to heaven, since from his perspective obedience to the law could not enable one to go to heaven.

There is simply no place in the Torah, or the rest of the Bible, or in the Talmud or in any other book of Judaism, that indicates that the Jews in the time of Jesus, before or since, ever believed that we needed to keep the laws of God in order to be justified, forgiven for our sins, to be made righteous, or to remove our guilt for our sins. The Jews never obeyed God's laws in order to get into heaven. Keeping God's laws brings heaven into the here and now.

Because we keep God's eternal laws, His commandments, it brings the Eternal God into our lives and puts us into a direct relationship with God as we obey Him.

Christianity begins with the belief that all are sinners and life begins with the taint of Original Sin; therefore, life begins with guilt. This belief in Original Sin and the sinful nature of man (as soon as he is able to choose his actions), require a channel for forgiveness or righteousness. Christian beliefs find this in the death of Jesus for the atonement of sins.

According to Judaism, our nature is not sinful (see Chapter 4, regarding Original Sin), and one does not become a sinner until one disobeys the commandments, until one disobeys Jewish law. We are not born with any guilt for any sin, and we do not obey God's laws to obtain forgiveness. I only need forgiveness if I disobey God's law. The need for forgiveness is preceded by the disobedience, and not the other way around.

Because Judaism rejects the idea of Original Sin, we have no need of Jesus, or God's law, to bring us forgiveness. We need God's laws to enhance our lives, to give structure and discipline to our lives. How one obtains forgiveness for sins and disobeying God's law, is discussed in Chapter 7 of this book.

Let us go back to my analogy of Jewish law and how it operates in Judaism. From the Jewish perspective, one does not obey the laws of driving to find forgiveness for speeding. According to the law, if one were to speed and get a ticket for speeding, it is the law itself that spells out how one gets forgiven for speeding, namely by paying the fine, or by taking a Defensive Driving course. One does not need forgiveness for speeding until one speeds.

5. That the Jewish Laws are too many for one person to obey, and that no one person can obey every law.

According to Jewish tradition, if someone took every single law in the Torah and counted them, regardless of what the law demanded, or from whom the law demanded obedience, one would find 613 commandments. This may sound like a lot of laws, but how many laws are on the books of the state in which you live? I am quite sure that there are more laws on the books of every single state in the United States, than the mere 613 laws found in the Torah. And yet almost everyone who reads this book will never have served a day in jail, or have been brought up on charges of breaking the laws of the city, county, or state in which they live.

One forgets that not every law in the Torah applies to every single person at every moment of their lives, just as the laws on the books of the state in which you live do not apply to you, every moment of your life.

Again, using the analogy of driving, if a person never drives an 18-wheeler truck, does this mean that they are guilty of not fulfilling the laws of driving a truck? Of course not, because the laws of driving a truck, which would still be listed in the collection of the laws of any state, do not apply to someone unless they get behind the wheel of a truck.

The same is true with God's laws. We are not expected to fulfill those laws that do not apply to us. If one is not a cohen, a priest, then the laws regarding priests in the Torah, part of the 613 laws, do not apply to that person. If one is a male, then the laws of women do not apply. If one does not live in the land of Israel, then the laws that only concern those who live in Israel do not apply. Truly, of the 613 laws found in the Torah, less than half will apply to any one person at any one time in his or her life. Even 300 laws may seem like a lot, but remember there are far more laws on the books of any one state that the citizens of that state follow without any problem.

Can a person be totally righteous in the eyes of God? The Bible speaks of two people who were. In Genesis we read about Noah:

> Genesis 6:9 *These are the generations of Noah. Noah was a righteous man, and perfect in his generations: Noah walked with God.*

And we also see the same thing regarding Job:

Job 1:1 *There was a man in the land of Uz, whose name was Job; and that man was perfect and upright, and one that feared God, and eschewed evil.*

Even the Bible believes that Jewish laws are doable. This is especially evident in the Torah:

Deuteronomy 30:11-14 For this commandment which I command thee this day, it is not hidden from thee, neither is it far off. 12 It is not in heaven, that thou shouldest say, Who shall go up for us to heaven, and bring it unto us, that we may hear it, and do it? 13 Neither is it beyond the sea, that thou shouldest say, Who shall go over the sea for us, and bring it unto us, that we may hear it, and do it? 14 But the word is very nigh unto thee, in thy mouth, and in thy heart, that thou mayest do it.

God tells us that the law is very doable. Rhetorically the passage above states that it is not hidden, it is not far away, it is not in heaven, it is not beyond the sea, but rather it is already here with us *that we may do it.* God states that we can do it, a sentiment that is absent when Paul refers to this passage in Romans 10:6-9:

But the righteousness which is of faith speaketh on this wise, Say not in thine heart, Who shall ascend into heaven? (that is, to bring Christ down from above:) 7 Or, Who shall descend into the deep? (That is, to bring up Christ again from the dead.) 8 But what saith it? The word is nigh thee, even in thy mouth, and in thy heart: that is, the word of faith, which we preach; 9 That if thou shalt confess with thy mouth the Lord Jesus, and shalt believe in thine heart that God hath raised him from the dead, thou shalt be saved.

Paul uses the passage from Deuteronomy 30 as a means to preach that one must believe in Jesus, because the law is not doable and has been superseded by faith in Jesus. To express this point, he leaves out the part of Deuteronomy 30:14 where God states "that you may do it."

As we said above, God would not give to anyone or to any group a set of laws that He knew could not be obeyed, and then condemn them for not obeying them. To do so would make God cruel.

6. That to break any one Jewish Law is the same as breaking any other law, and to break one law is to break them all

Many Christians believe that to break even one law of God in the Bible is the same as breaking every law. This concept is found in James 2:10:

> For whosoever shall keep the whole law, and yet offend in one point, he is guilty of all.

Of course, this is nonsense. Never did God in the Bible ever equate all laws to each other. This is simply shown by the punishments God gives out to those who break God's laws. One who steals does not receive the same penalty as one who commits first degree, pre-meditated, cold-blooded murder. Nor should they be the same. For murder, the Bible is clear,

> Exodus 21:12 *He that smiteth a man, so that he die, shall be surely put to death.*

And for stealing, the Bible is equally clear,

> Exodus 22:1 *If a man shall steal an ox, or a sheep, and kill it, or sell it; he shall restore five oxen for an ox, and four sheep for a sheep.*

Since the punishment meted out by God is different for the two transgressions, then in the eyes of God, they are not the same, and breaking one commandment is not as if one broke them all, or the punishment for every transgression, for every sin, would be the same, and that would mean the death penalty. This seems to be how Christianity understands this, however. Paul writes in Romans 6:23:

> For the wages of sin is death; but the gift of God is eternal life through Jesus Christ our Lord.

The wages of sin is not death. We die, and God created the world where, from the very beginning, death was an expected part of our existence (see Chapter 4 of this book).

This idea, that to break one law is to break them all, is absurd, and can be seen when we apply this attitude towards Jewish Law to the laws of driving.

First, if you are driving and you come to a school zone, you will slow down to 20 miles per hour or less. If you then entered the school zone, and looked down at the speedometer and saw that you were then going 23 miles per hour, are you speeding? Yes. To apply this Christian attitude towards Jewish Law to the laws of driving a car would mean that one should get the death penalty for going 23 in a school zone. If to break one law is to break them all, if, as Paul wrote, 'the wages of sin is death,' then one would get the death penalty for *any* transgression against the law, and so one would get the death penalty for going 23 in a 20 mile an hour school zone, as one would get the death penalty for cold-blooded murder.

Would a police officer give you a ticket for going 23 miles in a 20 mile an hour school zone? Most likely the officer would not.

Who is more compassionate, who is more merciful, and who is more understanding, a police officer, or God? God is more compassionate and merciful and understanding, and so God is ready to forgive faster than a human police officer.

Would a police officer be more likely to give you a ticket for going 23 in a school zone in August/September, or in May/June? I believe he would be more likely to do so in August/September, because he wants you to develop the right habits early in the school year. This explains why God seems to be so much stricter in the Biblical period than today.

Does God really expect perfection from us? God made us, and therefore knows, from the moment of our creation, that we are not perfect creatures. God knows that we will try but we will not always succeed. As a matter of fact, this is how God presents this in the Torah:

> Deuteronomy 6:3 *Hear therefore, O Israel, and observe to do it; that it may be well with thee, and that ye may increase mightily, as the Eternal God of thy fathers hath promised thee, in the land that floweth with milk and honey.*

The verse above states, "observe to do it." The Hebrew reads, "leesh-mor la-ah-sot." "Leesh-mor" means "to guard, to observe," and "la-ah-sot" means "to do." Does a guarded hen house get robbed of its chickens? Sometimes, yes! God knows we will try but not always succeed because we are not created as perfect creatures. To try our best is what God wants. If we stumble, as we will, if the guarded house gets robbed, and it will, God still loves us and forgives us when we follow the law to obtain and earn forgiveness (see Chapter 7 of this book).

What earns forgiveness? In Chapter 7 of this book, you will read that if we fast, if we pray for forgiveness, if we start obeying and stop disobeying then God will forgive us. In other words, our works, our deeds, and not our faith obtain for us forgiveness. While our faith may lead us to act, it is the actions that bring to us God's forgiveness.

How do we know what to do to earn God's forgiveness? Because the law itself tells us; just as civil law, for example, tells us how to be forgiven of a speeding ticket. We pay the fine; we take the defensive driving class; and, we don't do it again. If one does speed again, then the punishment will not be so lax, this time one might have to pay a bigger fine, or even go to jail rather than just take a defensive driving class.

On the other hand, as we read in our services every day, Deuteronomy 11:13-21 makes it sound as though to obey God's commandments insures that all will always be well with us, while to transgress the laws of God insures that all will go badly for us:

> *And it shall come to pass, if ye shall hearken diligently unto my commandments which I command you this day, to love the Eternal your God, and to serve him with all your heart and with all your soul, 14 That I will give you the rain of your land in his due season, the first rain and the latter rain, that thou mayest gather in thy corn, and thy wine, and thine oil. 15 And I will send grass in thy fields for thy cattle, that thou mayest eat and be full. 16 Take heed to yourselves, that your heart be not deceived, and ye turn aside, and serve other gods, and worship them; 17 And then the Eternal's wrath be kindled against you, and he shut up the heaven, that there be no rain, and that the land yield not her fruit; and lest ye perish quickly from off the good land which the Eternal giveth you. 18 Therefore shall ye lay up these my words in your heart and in your soul, and bind them for a sign upon your hand, that they may be as frontlets between your eyes. 19 And ye shall teach them your children, speaking of them when thou sittest in thine house, and when thou walkest by the way, when thou liest down, and when thou risest up. 20 And thou shalt write them upon the door posts of thine house, and upon thy gates: 21 That your days may be multiplied, and the days of your children, in the land which the Eternal swore unto your fathers to give them, as the days of heaven upon the earth.*

In other words, if you obey all will be Good, but if you disobey, all will be Bad. How real is this? Very real, as we learn from driving! Habits can kill, habits can lead to death. Running a stop sign, or drinking while driving, or running a red light will not always kill you or kill others, but if you keep doing it, the bad habit will catch up to you. Good habits can help you, and bad habits can hurt you.

Now, of course the obedience to God's laws will not insure a perfectly good life, just as disobedience to God's laws will not insure a horrible life. Bad things do happen to good people, and good does happen to those who are bad. However, the text is right, that over-all, one's life will more likely be better if one obeys and one's life will more likely be worse if one does not.

If a person is in the habit of not participating in faith, in religion, then how can their faith be there for them when times get rough? Religion is not running tap water, where one wants it to be there when one needs it, but will not pay for it and won't expend any effort to see to it that it is there when one gets thirsty. Everyone wants to just be able to go up to a faucet, take what you want and leave. Religion is not tap water; it requires us to have an ongoing relationship with our faith, in order for it to be able to help us when we need it.

Going back to our analogy of going 23 in a school zone, if you were to drive into a school zone and see that you were speeding, would you then pull over and give yourself up to the police, and expect the death penalty? Of course not, because the wages of speeding is not death. What you would do, and I suspect what you have done, is that you would simply just slow down and try not to do it again. The same is true with God's laws, and it is the same with Jewish law.

If I transgress God's law, I don't give up, become a pessimist, hate myself, or assume that it is simply the evil human nature to sin. I just try to do better. Judaism does not understand our occasional disobedience of God's laws as a statement about our nature, but rather it is a statement about our ability to do both Good and Bad, a constant choice that must be made between the two. Judaism does not emphasize the breaking of the law and our human capacity to sin, rather Judaism is joyful at our ability to choose to obey and to try to obey, and joyful at our successes. Judaism further believes that God, too, is joyful at our successes. This more positive attitude towards God and towards humanity generates greater self-esteem than emphasizing a sinful nature of man and a condemning God. It is therefore no wonder that Jews excel at so many things, since psychologists and studies show that a high self-esteem is important to success.

There is another reaction one might have, if one accepts the Christian attitude towards Jewish Law, that to break one law is the same as to break them all, and that the punishment of death is deserved for any transgression. If I see that I am going 23 in a 20 mile an hour school zone, I will then realize that I am breaking the law. I might say that since I am condemned anyway for going 23, then I may as well go 90 miles an hour. Why not? Since I cannot keep the law perfectly, I may as well not keep them at all. This leads us to the next misunderstanding of Jewish Law.

7. **That the observance or obedience to Jewish Law is an All-or-Nothing proposition**

Christianity seems to believe that for Jews, the obedience to God's laws is all or nothing. Sadly many Jews believe that the observance of Jewish Law is an all or nothing proposition, as well. Some believe that, since one must obey every Jewish law at all times, but does not (either by choice or by accident), then one either does not have to obey any Jewish Law.

Perhaps assimilating the Christian attitude towards Jewish Law, that to break one law is to break them all and that the penalty is the same for them all, many Jews feel that if they cannot do everything and at all times, they therefore choose to do nothing, or they choose to violate the law to a much greater extent.

Just because we are going to break Jewish law by going 23, does not give us permission to go 90. Let me explain.

The mindset that believes that since one cannot keep kosher in a restaurant that is not certified kosher anyway, then one may as well have the bacon cheeseburger is like the person who sees that he is going 23 in a 20 mile an hour school zone, and so he speeds through the school zone at 90. What this person fails to understand is that if one is going to break the law, then it is still better to break the law at a lesser level. As we said above, a human police officer most likely will not give someone a ticket for going 23, and God is far more compassionate and merciful than a human police officer. Of course the police would much prefer that one stays at 20 or below. Of course God would much prefer that we observe carefully and completely, all of God's laws, including the laws of keeping kosher. But as we also said above, these laws are not meant to condemn us, they are meant to make our lives better, and they were given to the Jewish People to make us better off. For our own sakes, we should observe these laws at least to some extent as best we can. We should choose only to go 23, if we are to break the law at all, rather than to go 90.

There are different levels of the Jewish Laws of keeping kosher.

First, there is the Biblical Laws found in Leviticus 11 that tells us which animals are kosher. There we are commanded not to eat anything from a pig, and to not eat anything in the waters unless it has both fins and scales. It is this latter commandment that precludes eating shellfish of any kind. Then there is the Rabbinic Laws that determine how the kosher animal is to be killed, prepared, and served. It is the observance of all these laws that make the food we eat kosher.

One's personal level of the observance of these laws of keeping kosher can vary on a very wide spectrum. One orthodox rabbi may not eat the food of another orthodox rabbi because the other rabbi's standard may be different than the first rabbi's standard, but they both, in fact, do keep kosher. A mashgiach is someone who sees to it that a restaurant or manufacturer maintains a certain standard of keeping kosher. However, the mashgiach for a restaurant may not, in fact, eat at that restaurant because his personal standards may be higher than the group for whom he works like the city's kosher certification organization. This does not mean that the food at that restaurant is not kosher, it just means that it is not at the personal level of that mashgiach. He did, after all, certify that restaurant as kosher, but at the city's level, and not at his own.

Similarly, one can keep kosher, even though it might be at a very low standard, but it is better to keep kosher at a lower standard than to not keep kosher at all.

When I go to a non-kosher fast-food restaurant, I have a choice. I can order a cheeseburger with bacon, I can order just the cheeseburger, I can order a hamburger, I can order a fish sandwich, and I can order a salad.

Do I really have to eat the bacon cheeseburger? I can recognize that God has commanded me not to eat pig, and I can choose, in response to God, not to eat the bacon. While it is true that the cheeseburger is combining dairy with meat, and the meat itself is not kosher beef, I am still responding to the commandment of God by refraining from eating the bacon on the sandwich. This means that, even on the lowest possible level, I am keeping kosher to an extent.

Here is a Chassidic story that exemplifies what I am trying to say.

Once, the disciples came to their Rabbi. They were playing stump-the-rabbi, and were trying to ask him a question to which there was no perfect answer. They asked him, "Rabbi, there is a ladder, and the ladder has 613 rungs on it. There is someone near the top, and someone near the bottom. Who, in the eyes of God, is higher?"

Now, the rabbi knew that the obvious answer to this would be the person near the top, who, being near the top observes nearly all of the 613 commandments. But to say that the person near the top is higher in the eyes of God would be presumptuous, and would deny the heights, however low, achieved by the one near the bottom. This, too, might dissuade someone near the bottom from climbing even higher. On the other hand the rabbi knew that to say the one near the bottom was higher in the eyes of God would be ludicrous, because of the heights obtained by the one near the top. So, the rabbi kept silent.

Thinking they had their rabbi stumped, they asked him, "Rabbi, what is the answer, if there is one?" He responded, "There is an answer, but you have not told me the whole story." The disciples said to him, "Certainly we have. There is a ladder with 613 rungs, someone is near the top, someone is near the bottom, and who in the eyes of God is higher?" And the rabbi said to them, "But you have not told me which of the two on the ladder is moving upwards?"

By making the choice for the cheeseburger, rather than for the bacon cheeseburger, you are placing yourself on the 613-runged ladder. Yes, you are near the bottom, but you have recognized that you have this ladder, whose purpose is to elevate you, to bring you closer to God, and to make your life more spiritual.

Yes, you are still eating dairy and meat together, and yes, you are eating meat that is not kosher, but because you are responding to the commandment of God by at least refraining from eating the bacon, you are keeping kosher, even if it is at the very lowest possible level.

Is it better to eat the cheeseburger than to eat the bacon cheeseburger? Yes, if you are doing so in response to God's commandments.

Is it even better to eat just the hamburger and not the cheeseburger? Yes, because it is a higher level of keeping kosher than eating the cheeseburger.

Is it better to not eat the hamburger, which is made of non-kosher beef, and to choose to eat the fish sandwich made of cod? Yes, because, again, you are climbing the 613-runged ladder with each choice.

Each Jewish law has its own merit, its own reward, and its own effect on the one who observes or obeys it. There is merit in choosing to not eat the bacon, even if the cheeseburger mixes dairy and meat, and even if the meat is not made of kosher beef. There is greater merit by not eating the bacon cheeseburger and not eating the cheeseburger, because now you are observing two different Jewish Laws. There is even greater merit by choosing to not eat the non-kosher meat and eating the fish sandwich of cod instead.

Every Jewish law has its own reward, and its own effect on the one who observes or obeys it.

I have asked someone what they do that is exclusively and distinctively Jewish, and why do they do it? Their answers could be categorized under four areas, and every single Jewish Law will fall under one or more of these four categories, as Dennis Prager described in the book he authored with Rabbi Joseph Telushkin, "The Nine Questions People Ask About Judaism: The Intelligent Skeptic's Guide." These categories are determined by the motivation of the one observing Jewish Law, and are not actually a category of the law itself.

These four categories are Holiness, Ethical, National, and Reflexive.

The first category is called Holiness. This means that what motivates a person to observe a Jewish Law is that it connects the person to God. It is a response to the Divine will, an acknowledgement that God has commanded. It is also an expression of making the act something that is spiritual. If one says that they are keeping kosher, to any extent, because God has commanded it, it means that every single time that person puts something in his or her mouth, he or she has to determine if it is kosher or not, and in keeping with what God has demanded. It means that the person, who keeps kosher for this reason, every time he or she eats, is reaffirming his or her relationship with God. It brings God into his or her life every time he or she eats.

The second category is called Ethical. This means that what motivates a person to observe Jewish Law is that it reminds the person to be ethical. Regarding keeping kosher, it means that he or she has chosen to keep kosher, to whatever extent, because he or she recognizes that Judaism demands the ethical treatment of animals, that the slaughtering of animals in the Jewish way is the most humane, and this is a constant concern of Judaism.

The third category is called National. This means that what motivates a person to observe a Jewish Law is that it connects the person to something else, another person, or to the Jewish People, and to something that is greater than the person alone. Regarding keeping kosher, it means that he or she keeps kosher to connect to the People who were commanded by God to refrain from eating pig or shellfish. It means that the person who has chosen to keep kosher, at whatever level, is part of something greater than himself or herself, and has connected to his or her 4,000 year old history.

The fourth category is called Reflexive. This means that what motivates a person to observe a Jewish Law is something that very directly affects the person observing it. Regarding keeping kosher, it means that the person has chosen for himself or herself, something that is a discipline regarding food. Psychology has shown us that those who are disciplined in one thing are a lot more likely to succeed at many things, while those who are disciplined at nothing are more likely to succeed at nothing. There is nothing harder to be disciplined in than in our eating habits. Anyone who has tried to lose weight knows this. By keeping kosher, even to a lesser extent, one becomes disciplined.

As I wrote above, any one Jewish Law will fall under one or more of these four categories. The more of these four categories that motivate a person to follow any one Jewish Law, the greater effect doing this law will have on their lives.

If a person wants to sense the Divine and bring God into his or her life; if a person wants to learn and practice the Ethical; if a person wants to connect not only with God, but also with the Jewish People who were commanded by God; if a person wants to do something that will make his or her life better for having done it; then, that person should seriously think about increasing his or her level of observance of Jewish Law. If a person wants to have all this in their lives, but who is not Jewish, they should seriously consider conversion to Judaism.

I was once told by a woman that she felt she had to stop lighting her Shabbat candles. I asked her why, and she told me that when she stopped keeping kosher in her home, she felt her home was no longer completely Jewish. She felt that lighting the Shabbat candles constituted a lie.

She said the glow of the Shabbat candles on her kitchen table made her feel as though God and her faith permeated her home. When she stopped keeping a kosher home, she felt that glow was a lie. After she heard me lecture on the topic of the myth that Judaism was a faith that believed the observance of Jewish Law was an all-or-nothing proposition, she told me I returned Shabbat candles to her home again.

8. That Jewish Laws become obsolete if one person perfectly obeys, or fulfills, those laws

In the Christian New Testament, in Matthew 5:17-18, Jesus is quoted as saying,

Think not that I am come to destroy the law, or the prophets: I am not come to destroy, but to fulfill. 18 For verily I say unto you, Till heaven and earth pass, one jot or one tittle shall in no wise pass from the law, till all be fulfilled.

Many Christians believe that this means that since Jesus supposedly fulfilled the law by doing them perfectly, that the Jewish Law given by God to the Jews through Moses have been made obsolete. This is not just wrong, it is simply absurd. Again, let me use the laws of driving a car to show why this is not correct.

If you are driving behind another car, and you both come to a stop sign, and the car in front of you perfectly obeys the laws of stopping at a stop sign, would this mean that the laws of stopping at a stop sign have been fulfilled and no one need stop at a stop sign again; obviously not.

The reason is that the laws of driving were not created in order to teach people that they will eventually break the laws of driving and, in turn, need the courts. The laws of driving were created to make the streets safer. They are for the benefit of the people, and not to condemn them. For example, if a stop light breaks, the law states that the intersection becomes like a four-way stop. All traffic in every direction must stop at the intersection, clear traffic, and then slowly pull forward through the intersection. This law makes driving safer and lets everyone know what is expected of them in this case.

Jewish Law is no different, and even if someone came along and obeyed every single law perfectly, even if it were God manifest in human form (a pagan idea as we have discussed in Chapter 2 of this book), the law would continue to be obeyed and would continue to help humanity as a result. Christianity believes that the laws were given by God to prepare the Jews for the coming of Jesus. So, when Jesus came, and supposedly fulfilled the laws, they became obsolete. However, since Jewish law was given by God to make the lives of those who follow them better off, the laws are eternal as God is eternal, because the benefit that comes from obeying God and God's laws will continue so long as they are obeyed.

9. That by punishing one person, another person's guilt for sins can be removed.

Although this will be discussed more fully in the Chapter 6, let me deal with it briefly with another analogy of traffic laws.

If I speed through a school zone and someone dies, God forbid, can someone else get the death penalty in my place, or go to jail in my place? Even if they volunteered to do so, would the courts allow it? Of course not. What if I was fined for my transgression, could someone else pay the fine? Actually, no. Someone else may give me the money to pay for the fine, but I am the one who is taken before the judge. I am the one who pleads guilty, and I am the one who has to pay the fine for my own guilt, regardless of where I get the money. The money becomes mine before I hand it over to the court.

CHAPTER 6

ONE PERSON DYING FOR THE SINS OF ANOTHER

Christianity teaches that the Messiah is a human sacrifice (that is, the blood sacrifice) necessary for the forgiveness of sin as we have discussed elsewhere. However, Jews are taught in our Bible that no one can die for the sins of another. This is told to us twice in the Torah and once in the Prophets.

In Exodus, Moses tries to offer himself as atonement for the sins of the people. Moses asks to be written out of God's book. We do not know what book of God's that may be, however to be written out of it means to be punished. Most believe this was the Book of Life, meaning the book in which God writes the names of those who will live through the next year, spoken of at the High Holy Days each year. This is what we mean when we wish each other at Rosh Hashanah, "may you be inscribed next year for a good year, L'shanah tovah tikatayvu." When Moses asked to be written out of the Book of Life, Moses was asking to die for the sins of the people. God's response was, "Whosoever hath sinned against me, him will I blot out of my book." God was saying, "No. It does not work this way. Each man must die for his own sin."

> Exodus 32:30-35 *And it came to pass on the morrow, that Moses said unto the people, Ye have sinned a great sin: and now I will go up unto the Eternal; perhaps I shall make an atonement for your sin. 31 And Moses returned unto the Eternal, and said, Oh, this people have sinned a*

great sin, and have made them gods of gold. 32 Yet now, if thou wilt forgive their sin—; and if not, blot me, I pray thee, out of thy book which thou hast written. 33 And the Eternal said unto Moses, Whosoever hath sinned against me, him will I blot out of my book. 34 Therefore now go, lead the people unto the place of which I have spoken unto thee: behold, mine Angel shall go before thee: nevertheless in the day when I visit I will visit their sin upon them. 35 And the Eternal plagued the people, because they made the calf, which Aaron made.

Then, in Deuteronomy, it summarizes this in a single verse:

Deuteronomy 24:16 The fathers shall not be put to death for the children, neither shall the children be put to death for the fathers: every man shall be put to death for his own sin.

In addition, the entirety of the eighteenth chapter of Ezekiel reaffirms this idea that no one can die for someone else's sin. Furthermore, Ezekiel 18 teaches that to be forgiven, human beings must simply stop doing the bad and start doing the good. Nowhere in Ezekiel 18 does it say that a blood sacrifice is required for the forgiveness of sins.

Ezekiel 18:1-4; 20-24; and 26-27 The word of the Eternal came unto me again, saying, 2 What mean ye, that ye use this proverb concerning the land of Israel, saying, The fathers have eaten sour grapes, and the children's teeth are set on edge? 3 As I live, saith the Eternal God, ye shall not have occasion any more to use this proverb in Israel. 4 Behold, all souls are mine; as the soul of the father, so also the soul of the son is mine: the soul that sinneth, it shall die . . . 20 The soul that sinneth, it shall die. The son shall not bear the iniquity of the father, neither shall the father bear the iniquity of the son: the righteousness of the righteous shall be upon him,

*and the wickedness of the wicked shall be upon him. 21
But if the wicked will turn from all his sins that he hath
committed, and keep all my statutes, and do that which is
lawful and right, he shall surely live, he shall not die. 22 All
his transgressions that he hath committed, they shall not be
mentioned unto him: in his righteousness that he hath done
he shall live. 23 Have I any pleasure at all that the wicked
should die? saith the Eternal God: and not that he should
return from his ways, and live? 24 But when the righteous
turneth away from his righteousness, and committeth
iniquity, and doeth according to all the abominations that
the wicked man doeth, shall he live? All his righteousness
that he hath done shall not be mentioned: in his trespass
that he hath trespassed, and in his sin that he hath sinned,
in them shall he die . . . 26 When a righteous man turneth
away from his righteousness, and committeth iniquity, and
dieth in them; for his iniquity that he hath done shall he
die. 27 Again, when the wicked man turneth away from his
wickedness that he hath committed, and doeth that which is
lawful and right, he shall save his soul alive.*

So, the Bible is clear and it is consistent, and there is no need for interpretation, no one can die for the sins of another.

Let us be clear regarding exactly what this means. If I sin, others may suffer as a result. But this does not mean that their suffering takes away my guilt. The only way I can remove my guilt is for me to repent of the sins I have committed. One generation may pollute the air, and the next generation may have to breathe that pollution into their lungs, but their coughing and deaths from lung cancer will not remove the guilt of the generation that polluted. It is one thing to say that someone else suffers as a result of another's sins, but it is a totally different thing to say, and a very unbiblical thing to say, that one's suffering or even one's death takes the guilt away from, and renders sinless, someone else.

Furthermore, one person may sacrifice his or her life for the life of another. We know of soldiers who will throw their bodies onto a live hand grenade to save the lives of his or her companions. However, this does not mean that soldier's death removed any guilt from any sins that may have been committed by the soldiers he saved.

Jesus cannot die for anyone else's sin. Jesus cannot die for the sins of another person because it is antithetical to what the Bible says.

If a person commits first degree, cold-blooded, premeditated murder, another person cannot tell the court, "I didn't commit this crime, but murder me instead of the person who did." A court would never allow this, but Christianity does so by saying that Jesus can die for others' sins.

Jesus' disciples also knew that one person could not die for the sins of another, much less for the sins of humanity. The disciples did not have a concept of a dying/saving Messiah. When Jesus tried to explain that this was his mission, and his definition of what it meant to be a Messiah, the disciples' response was disbelief, they did not understand, and they rebuked Jesus for saying it.

> Matthew 16:13-23 *When Jesus came into the coasts of Caesarea Philippi, he asked his disciples, saying, Whom do men say that I the Son of man am? 14 And they said, Some say that thou art John the Baptist: some, Elias; and others, Jeremias, or one of the prophets. 15 He saith unto them, But whom say ye that I am? 16 And Simon Peter answered and said, Thou art the Christ, the Son of the living God. 17 And Jesus answered and said unto him, Blessed art thou, Simon Barjona: for flesh and blood hath not revealed it unto thee, but my Father which is in heaven. 18 And I say also unto thee, That thou art Peter, and upon this rock I will build my church; and the gates of hell shall not prevail against it. 19 And I will give unto thee the keys of the kingdom of heaven: and whatsoever thou shalt bind on earth shall be bound in heaven: and whatsoever thou shalt loose on earth shall be loosed in heaven. 20 Then charged he his disciples that they should tell no man that he was Jesus the Christ. 21 From that time forth began Jesus to show unto his disciples,*

how that he must go unto Jerusalem, and suffer many things of the elders and chief priests and scribes, and be killed, and be raised again the third day. 22 Then Peter took him, and began to rebuke him, saying, Be it far from thee, Lord: this shall not be unto thee. 23 But he turned, and said unto Peter, Get thee behind me, Satan: thou art an offence unto me: for thou savourest not the things that be of God, but those that be of men.

This story is also repeated in both Mark and in Luke.

Mark 8:31-33 And he began to teach them, that the Son of man must suffer many things, and be rejected of the elders, and of the chief priests, and scribes, and be killed, and after three days rise again. 32 And he spoke that saying openly. And Peter took him, and began to rebuke him. 33 But when he had turned about and looked on his disciples, he rebuked Peter, saying, Get thee behind me, Satan: for thou savourest not the things that be of God, but the things that be of men.

Luke 18:31-34 Then he took unto him the twelve, and said unto them, Behold, we go up to Jerusalem, and all things that are written by the prophets concerning the Son of man shall be accomplished. 32 For he shall be delivered unto the Gentiles, and shall be mocked, and spitefully entreated, and spitted on: 33 And they shall scourge him, and put him to death: and the third day he shall rise again. 34And they understood none of these things: and this saying was hid from them, neither knew they the things which were spoken.

Had Jesus' disciples understood that the Messiah was to die for the sins of humanity, when Jesus told them his mission, they would have rejoiced and cried out that their salvation had arrived. Instead they rebuke Jesus for saying such a thing!

The idea that one person could die for another's sins, or the concept of a dying/saving Messiah was not known in Judaism even in the time of Jesus, but it was a concept found all over the ancient pagan world.

CHAPTER 7

THE NECESSITY OF A BLOOD SACRIFICE

The idea that a blood sacrifice is required for the forgiveness of sins is a very common assumption within Christianity. Paul writes that there is no remission of sin without a blood sacrifice:

> Hebrews 9:22 *And almost all things are by the law purged with blood; and without shedding of blood is no remission.*

Christians believe that one needs a blood sacrifice for the forgiveness of sin and that one who does not have a blood sacrifice will die in their sins and go to hell. For Christians, the ultimate and only blood sacrifice that counts with God came in the death of Jesus. Christianity believes that if one does not accept the death of Jesus as one's blood sacrifice, then one is condemned to an eternity enduring the punishments of hell.

> John 3:36 *He that believeth on the Son hath everlasting life: and he that believeth not the Son shall not see life; but the wrath of God abideth on him.*

However, this is not an assumption made by the Bible or by Judaism. The God-man relationship was never limited to the animal sacrifices, nor was it ever the only means by which a human being obtained forgiveness from God for sin.

The centrality of the animal sacrifices ceased, not with the second destruction of the Temple by the Romans, but rather with the first destruction of the Temple by the Babylonians. One must keep in mind that the vast majority of Jews never returned to the Promised Land under Cyrus of Persia. They remained in Babylonia. By the time Jesus was born, eighty percent of the world's Jewish community lived outside the Promised Land, and did not care about the cessation of animal sacrifices. When the Temple was reestablished, the Jews of Babylonia made an annual financial gift for the maintenance of the Temple and the land, but never worried that God would not forgive them their sins without a blood sacrifice (much as Jews all over the world do today). They had no such fear because the Bible makes it explicitly clear that no blood sacrifice is necessary for the forgiveness of sins. The Bible also makes it clear that an animal sacrifice is not the exclusive means of obtaining forgiveness.

The book of Jonah proves that blood sacrifices are unnecessary. Jonah tries to escape from doing God's will of preaching to the people of Ninevah. After the problem with the great fish, he goes to the people of Ninevah, says five words to them (in the original Hebrew) as we read in the third chapter:

> Jonah 3:4 *And Jonah began to enter into the city a day's journey, and he cried, and said, Yet forty days, and Nineveh shall be overthrown.*

After the King and subjects heard Jonah's short prophecy to them, what did they do?

> *7 And he caused it to be proclaimed and published through Ninevah, by the decree of the King and his nobles, saying, Let neither man nor beast, herd nor flock taste anything; let them not feed nor drink water; 8 but let man and beast be covered with sackcloth, and cry mightily unto God; yea, let them turn everyone from his evil way, and from the violence that is in their hands. 9 Who can tell if*

God will turn and repent, and turn away from his fierce anger that we perish not? 10 And God saw their works, that they turned from their evil way; and God repented of the evil, that he had said that he would do unto them; and he did not do it.

In verse 10, above, Jonah tells us that God saw their *works*, their deeds, how they turned from their evil ways, and God forgave them. It does not say God saw their blood sacrifice, because they never offered one. It does not say that it was only their faith that saved them, but rather the works that it led them to do. God saw their deeds. They fasted ("let neither man nor beast, herd nor flock, taste anything. Let them not feed or drink water," Jonah 3:7), they prayed ("Let them cry mightily to God," Jonah 3:8), and they stopped doing evil and started doing good ("Let everyone turn from his evil ways and from the violence which is in his hands," Jonah 3:8). What was God's response? God forgives them of their sins because of their works ("When God saw what they did, how they turned from their evil way, God repented of the Evil which He had said He would do unto them, and He did not do it," Jonah 3:10). It is because of all this that Jews read the book of Jonah each Yom Kippur afternoon, the Day of Atonement, the very day each year when Judaism emphasizes our need to repent of our sins, and to seek forgiveness from others first, so that we can seek, and find, forgiveness from God. And we Jews do what the People of Ninevah did, we fast, we pray, and we stop doing the sin and we start doing good, and the Book of Jonah promises us that this is all that is necessary for God to forgive us.

There are plenty of other examples that show a blood sacrifice is not necessary for God to forgive us for our sins. However, showing only one instance where God did not demand a blood sacrifice, as we saw above in Jonah, proves blood sacrifices are not necessary for the forgiveness of sins. This sharply contrasts the Christian belief that, to be forgiven for their sins, human beings need the blood sacrifice of Jesus.

Many people often tell the Jews they remain guilty for their sins, having no Temple in which to make sacrifices. They claim that, without the shedding of blood, there is no forgiveness, there is no remission of sin, as we read above from Hebrews 9:22.

But is this true? Must blood be shed to obtain forgiveness? Those who believe that one must have a blood sacrifice for the forgiveness of sins often cite Leviticus 17:11, which reads:

> *For the life of the flesh is in the blood: and I have given*
> *it to you upon the altar to make an atonement for your souls:*
> *for it is the blood that maketh an atonement for the soul.*

If it were true that it is the blood that makes atonement, then one might believe that it is only through a sacrifice involving blood that one can obtain forgiveness for one's sins. However, if you read the whole verse in context, you will find that it refers to abstaining from eating the blood of a sacrifice, and nothing more. God commands the abstention from eating or drinking blood because most other pagan religions consumed the blood of their sacrifices as a way of incorporating their gods into their bodies and into their lives.

This is similar to the Christian ritual of communion where the body and blood of Jesus are consumed in the wine and in the bread. However, the holiness of the people of Israel prohibits them from practicing such pagan rituals and holding the same beliefs as their pagan neighbors. The entire quotation from Leviticus 17:10-14 reads:

> *And whatsoever man there be of the house of Israel,*
> *or of the strangers that sojourn among you, that eateth any*
> *manner of blood; I will even set my face against that soul*
> *that eateth blood, and will cut him off from among his*
> *people. 11 For the life of the flesh is in the blood: and I*
> *have given it to you upon the altar to make an atonement*
> *for your souls: for it is the blood that maketh an atonement*
> *for the soul. 12 Therefore I said unto the children of Israel,*
> *No soul of you shall eat blood, neither shall any stranger*
> *that sojourneth among you eat blood. 13 And whatsoever*
> *man there be of the children of Israel, or of the strangers*

*that sojourn among you, which hunteth and catcheth any
beast or fowl that may be eaten; he shall even pour out the
blood thereof, and cover it with dust. 14 For it is the life
of all flesh; the blood of it is for the life thereof: therefore I
said unto the children of Israel, Ye shall eat the blood of no
manner of flesh: for the life of all flesh is the blood thereof:
whosoever eateth it shall be cut off.*

There are many examples in the Bible, where things other than
blood are used to make atonement for sins. Those who were poor
and unable to afford a blood sacrifice are allowed by God to use
flour, which has no blood and no life.

*Leviticus 5:11-13 If, however, he cannot afford two
doves or two young pigeons, he is to bring as an offering for
his sin a tenth of an ephah of fine flour for a sin offering. He
must not put oil or incense on it, because it is a sin offering.
He is to bring it to the priest, who shall take a handful of
it as a memorial portion and burn it on the altar on top of
the offerings made to the Eternal by fire. It is a sin offering.
In this way the priest will make atonement for him for any
of these sins he has committed, and he will be forgiven. The
rest of the offering will belong to the priest, as in the case of
the grain offering.*

If a blood sacrifice were absolutely necessary for the forgiveness
of sin, then even the poor man would have had to have brought a
blood sacrifice for his sins. By allowing him to bring flour, with no
blood and no life to be offered, the Bible clearly states that a blood
sacrifice was not absolutely necessary, even if it was, indeed, one of
the ways one could obtain forgiveness. Again, as we stated above, if
we could show even only one time in the Bible that forgiveness was
given by God without a blood sacrifice, then it would prove that
they were not absolutely necessary for God to forgive us. As we have
already seen there were and are many examples. Here, just offering
incense was enough:

> Numbers 16:47 *So Aaron did as Moses said, and*
> *ran into the midst of the assembly. The plague had already*
> *started among the people, but Aaron offered the incense and*
> *made atonement for them.*

In the following verse, jewelry is offered for atonement, but no blood is shed.

> Numbers 31:50 *So we have brought as an offering to*
> *the Eternal the gold articles each of us acquired—armlets,*
> *bracelets, signet rings, earrings and necklaces—to make*
> *atonement for ourselves before the Eternal.*

In the following, silver or money is offered for atonement, but no blood is shed:

> Exodus 30:15-16 *The rich shall not give more, and*
> *the poor shall not give less than half a shekel, when they*
> *give an offering unto the Eternal, to make an atonement for*
> *your souls. And thou shalt take the atonement money of the*
> *children of Israel, and shalt appoint it for the service of the*
> *tabernacle of the congregation; that it may be a memorial*
> *unto the children of Israel before the Eternal, to make an*
> *atonement for your souls.*

There are more examples of other means to God's forgiveness without using a blood sacrifice.

Another superior method of atonement is charity.

"Charity" is usually the translation given for the Hebrew word "tzedakah." However, a more accurate translation of the word "tzedakah" would be the word "righteousness." Charity/righteousness can be used to obtain forgiveness from God, as we read from the Bible. This is stated often in the Book of Proverbs:

> 10:2 *Treasures of wickedness profit nothing: but*
> *righteousness (tzedakah) delivereth from death.*

11:4 *Riches profit not in the day of wrath: but righteousness (tzedakah) delivereth from death.*

16:6 *By mercy and truth iniquity is purged: and by the fear of the Eternal men depart from evil.*

21:3 *To do justice (tzedakah) and judgment is more acceptable to the Eternal than sacrifice.*

And as the prophet Daniel taught to the King,

Daniel 4:27 *Wherefore, O king, let my counsel be acceptable unto thee, and break off thy sins by righteousness (tzedakah), and thine iniquities by showing mercy to the poor; if it may be a lengthening of thy tranquility.*

Based on these verses, it is obvious that a blood sacrifice is not needed. In the following verses, Isaiah has his sin removed by a live coal:

Isaiah 6:6-7 *Then flew one of the seraphim unto me, having a live coal in his hand, which he had taken with the tongs from off the altar: 7 And he laid it upon my mouth, and said, Lo, this hath touched thy lips; and thine iniquity is taken away, and thy sin purged.*

It is true that without a Temple, Jews cannot offer any kind of blood sacrifice. This is why God gave the Jews many methods of atonement. There was a time in Israel's history when the people were consumed with sacrificial ceremonies. God rebuked them for this and reminded them that the laws of God are more important than the sacrifices.

Jeremiah 7:22-23 *For I spoke not unto your fathers, nor commanded them in the day that I brought them out of the land of Egypt, concerning burnt offerings or sacrifices:*

23 But this thing commanded I them, saying, Obey my voice, and I will be your God, and ye shall be my people: and walk ye in all the ways that I have commanded you, that it may be well unto you.

Out of all the methods God gave the Jews for atonement, the sacrifices were the weakest. This is true because sacrifices only made atonement for one kind of sin. Missionary Christians often try to point out verses that demonstrate a need for sacrifices as atonement for sins. However, they fail to mention that only unintentional sins are forgiven by blood sacrifices. Note in the verses quoted below, that they all refer only to sins which were unintentional, which were done in ignorance, and they precede a description of a blood sacrifice:

Leviticus 4:1-2 *And the Eternal spoke unto Moses, saying, 2 Speak unto the children of Israel, saying, If a soul shall sin through ignorance against any of the commandments of the Eternal concerning things which ought not to be done, and shall do against any of them:*

Leviticus 4:13 *And if the whole congregation of Israel sin through ignorance, and the thing be hid from the eyes of the assembly, and they have done somewhat against any of the commandments of the Eternal concerning things which should not be done, and are guilty;*

Leviticus 4:22 *When a ruler hath sinned, and done somewhat through ignorance against any of the commandments of the Eternal his God concerning things which should not be done, and is guilty;*

Leviticus 4:27 *And if any one of the common people sin through ignorance, while he doeth somewhat against any of the commandments of the Eternal concerning things which ought not to be done, and be guilty;*

Leviticus 5:15 *If a soul commit a trespass, and sin through ignorance, in the holy things of the Eternal; then he shall bring for his trespass unto the Eternal a ram without blemish out of the flocks, with thy estimation by shekels of silver, after the shekel of the sanctuary, for a trespass offering:*

Leviticus 5:18 *And he shall bring a ram without blemish out of the flock, with thy estimation, for a trespass offering, unto the priest: and the priest shall make an atonement for him concerning his ignorance wherein he erred and wist it not, and it shall be forgiven him.*

Numbers 15:22 *And if ye have erred, and not observed all these commandments, which the Eternal hath spoken unto Moses,*

Numbers 15:24-29 *Then it shall be, if ought be committed by ignorance without the knowledge of the congregation, that all the congregation shall offer one young bullock for a burnt offering, for a sweet savour unto the Eternal, with his meat offering, and his drink offering, according to the manner, and one kid of the goats for a sin offering. 25 And the priest shall make an atonement for all the congregation of the children of Israel, and it shall be forgiven them; for it is ignorance: and they shall bring their offering, a sacrifice made by fire unto the Eternal, and their sin offering before the Eternal, for their ignorance: 26 And it shall be forgiven all the congregation of the children of Israel, and the stranger that sojourneth among them; seeing all the people were in ignorance. 27 And if any soul sin through ignorance, then he shall bring a she goat of the first year for a sin offering. 28 And the priest shall make an atonement for the soul that sinneth ignorantly, when he sinneth by ignorance before the Eternal, to make an atonement for him; and it shall be forgiven him. 29 Ye*

shall have one law for him that sinneth through ignorance,
both for him that is born among the children of Israel, and
for the stranger that sojourneth among them.

Because the sin was not done intentionally, the priest brought to the Eternal an offering made by fire, and a sin offering. The entire Israelite community and the aliens living among them are forgiven, because all the people were involved in the unintentional wrong.

However, if someone commits a sin intentionally, the one who committed the sin will be punished, and not an animal.

Numbers 15:30-31 *But the soul that doeth ought presumptuously, whether he be born in the land, or a stranger, the same reproacheth the Eternal; and that soul shall be cut off from among his people. 31 Because he hath despised the word of the Eternal, and hath broken his commandment, that soul shall utterly be cut off; his iniquity shall be upon him.*

For some intentional sins, the punishment is severe.

Numbers 15:32-36 *And while the children of Israel were in the wilderness, they found a man that gathered sticks upon the sabbath day. 33 And they that found him gathering sticks brought him unto Moses and Aaron, and unto all the congregation. 34 And they put him in ward, because it was not declared what should be done to him. 35 And the Eternal said unto Moses, The man shall be surely put to death: all the congregation shall stone him with stones without the camp. 36 And all the congregation brought him without the camp, and stoned him with stones, and he died; as the Eternal commanded Moses.*

For someone to atone for an intentional sin, there must be repentance and restitution. Punishment is also necessary if the sin is committed intentionally.

Exodus 22:1-14 *If a man shall steal an ox, or a sheep, and kill it, or sell it; he shall restore five oxen for an ox, and four sheep for a sheep. 2 If a thief be found breaking up, and be smitten that he die, there shall no blood be shed for him. 3 If the sun be risen upon him, there shall be blood shed for him; for he should make full restitution; if he have nothing, then he shall be sold for his theft. 4 If the theft be certainly found in his hand alive, whether it be ox, or ass, or sheep; he shall restore double. 5 If a man shall cause a field or vineyard to be eaten, and shall put in his beast, and shall feed in another man's field; of the best of his own field, and of the best of his own vineyard, shall he make restitution. 6 If fire break out, and catch in thorns, so that the stacks of corn, or the standing corn, or the field, be consumed therewith; he that kindled the fire shall surely make restitution. 7 If a man shall deliver unto his neighbour money or stuff to keep, and it be stolen out of the man's house; if the thief be found, let him pay double. 8 If the thief be not found, then the master of the house shall be brought unto the judges, to see whether he have put his hand unto his neighbour's goods. 9 For all manner of trespass, whether it be for ox, for ass, for sheep, for raiment, or for any manner of lost thing, which another challengeth to be his, the cause of both parties shall come before the judges; and whom the judges shall condemn, he shall pay double unto his neighbour. 10 If a man deliver unto his neighbour an ass, or an ox, or a sheep, or any beast, to keep; and it die, or be hurt, or driven away, no man seeing it: 11 Then shall an oath of the Eternal be between them both, that he hath not put his hand unto his neighbour's goods; and the owner of it shall accept thereof, and he shall not make it good. 12 And if it be stolen from him, he shall make restitution unto the owner thereof. 13 If it be torn in pieces, then let him bring it for witness, and he shall not make good that which was torn. 14 And if a man borrow ought of his neighbour, and it be hurt, or die, the owner thereof being not with it, he shall surely make it good.*

Leviticus 24:21 *And he that killeth a beast, he shall restore it: and he that killeth a man, he shall be put to death.*

Numbers 5:6-7 *Speak unto the children of Israel, When a man or woman shall commit any sin that men commit, to do a trespass against the Eternal, and that person be guilty; 7 Then they shall confess their sin which they have done: and he shall recompense his trespass with the principal thereof, and add unto it the fifth part thereof, and give it unto him against whom he hath trespassed.*

Other methods of atonement are superior to the sacrificial system because they can be used to obtain forgiveness from God for any sin, and not just unintentional ones. God truly desires Teshuva from us, which means "repentance" and "return" to God.

2 Chronicles 7:14 *If my people, which are called by my name, shall humble themselves, and pray, and seek my face, and turn from their wicked ways; then will I hear from heaven, and will forgive their sin, and will heal their land.*

Deuteronomy 4:29 *But if from thence thou shalt seek the Eternal thy God, thou shalt find him, if thou seek him with all thy heart and with all thy soul.*

Job 33:26 *He shall pray unto God, and he will be favourable unto him: and he shall see his face with joy: for he will render unto man his righteousness.*

Psalm 34:14 *Depart from evil, and do good; seek peace, and pursue it.*

Psalm 34:18 *The Eternal is nigh unto them that are of a broken heart; and saveth such as be of a contrite spirit.*

The following verse also demonstrates that God wants true repentance and prayer from us—*not* sacrifice.

> Psalm 51:16-17 *For thou desirest not sacrifice; else would I give it: thou delightest not in burnt offering. 17 The sacrifices of God are a broken spirit: a broken and a contrite heart, O God, thou wilt not despise.*

Remember, the Psalms were written to sing praises to God in the Temple, right where the sacrifices themselves were offered. The psalmists understood quite well God's attitude toward the sacrifices.

> Psalm 40:6 *Sacrifice and offering thou didst not desire; mine ears hast thou opened: burnt offering and sin offering hast thou not required.*

God wants us simply to pray sincerely for forgiveness. In fact, prayer replaces the sacrifices, just as God commands in Hosea 14:1-2:

> *1 O Israel, return unto the Eternal thy God; for thou hast fallen by thine iniquity. 2 Take with you words, and turn to the Eternal: say unto him, Take away all iniquity, and receive us graciously: so will we render the calves of our lips.*

Please note that many Christian translations mistranslate this passage. The Hebrew is quite clear—"Pa-reem S'fa-tay-nu" means "the bulls of our lips." Instead, the Hebrew is often mistranslated as if it said "Pay-rote S'fa-tay-nu," which means "the fruit of our lips." Such translations change the word of God. God accepts prayer in place of sacrifices because the "bulls of our lips," the sacrifices we offer, like bulls, are the prayers that come out of our mouths.

> Proverbs 28:13 *He that covereth his sins shall not prosper: but whoso confesseth and forsaketh them shall have mercy.*

Hosea 6:6 *For I desired mercy, and not sacrifice; and the knowledge of God more than burnt offerings.*

Please note that the following quotations all come from I Kings 8, in which King Solomon dedicates the only Temple in the world to the one true God. Even though the Temple was to be the center of the worship of the one true God, even though this was to be the place where all sacrifices to God were to be made, Solomon himself knew that God did not require blood sacrifices for the forgiveness of sin. Therefore, at the dedication of this very Temple, Solomon asks that one need only pray to God for forgiveness, after repenting, and God forgives. If Solomon thought that a blood sacrifice was absolutely necessary, he would not have asked.

1 Kings 8:38-39 *What prayer and supplication soever be made by any man, or by all thy people Israel, which shall know every man the plague of his own heart, and spread forth his hands toward this house: 39 Then hear thou in heaven thy dwelling place, and forgive, and do, and give to every man according to his ways, whose heart thou knowest; (for thou, even thou only, knowest the hearts of all the children of men).*

The Gentiles too, are to pray directly to God for the forgiveness of their sins, and without the need of a sacrifice:

1 Kings 8:41-43 *Moreover concerning a stranger, that is not of thy people Israel, but cometh out of a far country for thy name's sake; 42 (For they shall hear of thy great name, and of thy strong hand, and of thy stretched out arm;) when he shall come and pray toward this house; 43 Hear thou in heaven thy dwelling place, and do according to all that the stranger calleth to thee for: that all people of the earth may know thy name, to fear thee, as do thy people Israel; and that they may know that this house, which I have builded, is called by thy name.*

God allows the Gentiles to pray directly to God, without the need of a mediator. God never excludes anyone from Him. All God asks for is a contrite heart and the willingness to follow Him.

Remember still, that the whole of the sacrificial system was centered at the Temple. Solomon continues:

> 1 Kings 8:46-50 *If they sin against thee, (for there is no man that sinneth not,) and thou be angry with them, and deliver them to the enemy, so that they carry them away captives unto the land of the enemy, far or near; 47 Yet if they shall bethink themselves in the land whither they were carried captives, and repent, and make supplication unto thee in the land of them that carried them captives, saying, We have sinned, and have done perversely, we have committed wickedness; 48 And so return unto thee with all their heart, and with all their soul, in the land of their enemies, which led them away captive, and pray unto thee toward their land, which thou gavest unto their fathers, the city which thou hast chosen, and the house which I have built for thy name: 49 Then hear thou their prayer and their supplication in heaven thy dwelling place, and maintain their cause, 50 And forgive thy people that have sinned against thee, and all their transgressions wherein they have transgressed against thee, and give them compassion before them who carried them captive, that they may have compassion on them.*

This means that if you do Teshuva, if you repent, if you pray for forgiveness, then God will forgive you, and restore your righteousness even though you sinned.

> Job 33:26-28 *He shall pray unto God, and he will be favourable unto him: and he shall see his face with joy: for he will render unto man his righteousness. 27 He looketh upon men, and if any say, I have sinned, and perverted that which was right, and it profited me not; 28 He will*

deliver his soul from going into the pit, and his life shall see the light.

God has clearly shown us that sacrifice is not necessary for atonement. God makes it abundantly clear to Israel what we are to do for atonement. The idea that one must have a blood sacrifice for the forgiveness of sin is simply not Biblical.

> Micah 6:6-8 *Wherewith shall I come before the Eternal, and bow myself before the high God? shall I come before him with burnt offerings, with calves of a year old? 7 Will the Eternal be pleased with thousands of rams, or with ten thousands of rivers of oil? shall I give my firstborn for my transgression, the fruit of my body for the sin of my soul? 8 He hath shewed thee, O man, what is good; and what doth the Eternal require of thee, but to do justly, and to love mercy, and to walk humbly with thy God?*

One could ask that if God never stated that blood sacrifices were absolutely necessary for the forgiveness of sin, why did God make the sacrificial system so detailed, and why was there, then, a need for a Temple at all?

The reason is that in the ancient world, the pagans would sacrifice anything, or anybody, to any god, anywhere. God wanted one people, His people, to not have blood sacrifices as the central means to worship Him, and so He weaned His people away from them. However, this had to be done slowly over time. God first limited the blood sacrifices to exclude human sacrifices in Genesis, which we learn from the Binding of Isaac, and again in Deuteronomy where God called human sacrifice an abomination to Him and something He hates, as we shall see in the next chapter. God then limited what kinds of animals could be used in Leviticus. Then God further limited the sacrifices by stating they could only be done at the Temple, and then God ultimately got rid of the Temple. This process took many hundreds of years, slowly weaning the Jews away from blood sacrifices.

CHAPTER 8

GOD ACCEPTING A HUMAN SACRIFICE

Christians believe that Jesus was a blood sacrifice who saves all human beings from their sin. If this is true, one must consider who exactly died on the cross. If it was Jesus the God, Christians are forced to explain how God could die. On the other hand, if it was only Jesus the human who died, Christians are left with nothing more than a human sacrifice. And what, exactly, does God say about human sacrifice in the Bible?

Much of Deuteronomy is devoted to commanding the Jews to not become like the people who then inhabited the Promised Land. Up until Deuteronomy, when the Israelites are preparing to enter the land, they rubbed elbows, so to speak, only with their own community. Now, however, when they enter the Promised Land, they will be learning about the indigenous population. God, in Deuteronomy tells them repeatedly not to become like the pagan idolaters living in the land. In Deuteronomy 12, God tells the Jews not to be like those who live in the Promised Land, and explicitly calls human sacrifice something that He hates, and that is an abomination to Him.

> Deuteronomy 12:30-31 *Take heed to thyself that thou be not snared by following them, after that they be destroyed from before thee; and that thou inquire not after their gods, saying, How did these nations serve their gods? even so will I do likewise. 31 Thou shalt not do so unto*

> *the Eternal thy God: for every abomination to the Eternal, which he hateth, have they done unto their gods; for even their sons and their daughters they have burnt in the fire to their gods.*

In Jeremiah, the Jews had become like the peoples around them, and had become involved in human sacrifices. Here in Jeremiah, God tells us that human sacrifice is so horrible a concept that He did not even think to command such a thing:

> Jeremiah 19:4-6 *Because they have forsaken me, and have estranged this place, and have burned incense in it unto other gods, whom neither they nor their fathers have known, nor the kings of Judah, and have filled this place with the blood of innocents; 5 They have built also the high places of Baal, to burn their sons with fire for burnt offerings unto Baal, which I commanded not, nor spoke it, neither came it into my mind: 6 Therefore, behold, the days come, saith the Eternal, that this place shall no more be called Tophet, nor The Valley of the Son of Hinnom, but The Valley of Slaughter.*

The same concept is found in Psalm 106 and in Ezekiel 16.

> Psalm 106:37-38 *Yea, they sacrificed their sons and their daughters unto devils, And shed innocent blood, even the blood of their sons and of their daughters, whom they sacrificed unto the idols of Canaan: and the land was polluted with blood. 38 And shed innocent blood, even the blood of their sons and of their daughters, whom they sacrificed unto the idols of Canaan: and the land was polluted with blood.*

> Ezekiel 16:20-21 *Moreover thou hast taken thy sons and thy daughters, whom thou hast borne unto me, and these hast thou sacrificed unto them to be devoured. Is this*

of thy whoredoms a small matter, 21 That thou hast slain my children, and delivered them to cause them to pass through the fire for them?

In spite of all this, are we now to believe that God requires human sacrifice? Are we to further believe that God wants the sacrifice of His own human son? After telling the Jews to reject pagan practices and pagan beliefs, why would God then change His mind and say, "Okay, now go ahead and believe in a human sacrifice, just as these very pagans believe? And not only that; but the human in whose death I want you to believe will be my very own son?" When did God change His mind?

Christians define the Messiah exactly as the pagans understood their dying/saving man/gods and heroes. The ancient world is filled with examples that support this idea. Many gods were born in the winter, died in the spring, and came back to life, concurrent with the belief that their followers would not die, but have immortal life, because the death of the dying/saving man/god acts as a sacrifice for the sins of the people. The pagan world is filled with beings that were the products of a human mother with a divine father, such as Hercules or Dionysus, whose father was Zeus and whose mothers were human.

Christians teach that Jesus was crucified at Passover as a type of lamb, whose spilled blood would atone for the sins of the world. In the New Testament, this is how Jesus is portrayed:

John 1:29 *The next day John seeth Jesus coming unto him, and saith, Behold the Lamb of God, which taketh away the sin of the world.*

Although this should be obvious, Jesus was a human being, and not a lamb. Christians may believe that Jesus was also God; however for there to have been a death on the cross, it had to be Jesus-the-human that died, and not Jesus-the-God who died, since the One True God cannot die.

The sacrifice of the Passover lamb is not a very good foreshadowing of the death of Jesus. The lamb at Passover is not a sin sacrifice, but Christians consider the death of Jesus to have been a sin sacrifice. According to the Bible, the sacrifice of the Passover lamb was so that the blood of the Passover lamb could be used to mark the doorposts. In this way God would know which house was Jewish and which house was not, for the Plague of the Smiting of the Firstborn (Exodus 12:13, 23).

Furthermore, the Passover sacrifice, like all sacrifices, was to have been without any blemish as it states in Exodus 12:5:

> *Your lamb shall be without blemish, a male of the first*
> *year; ye shall take it from the sheep, or from the goats;*

Jesus would have been disqualified almost from birth because, according to Paul, Jesus was as good as castrated. Paul likens circumcision to partial castration, and suggests that those who believe in circumcision that were troubling his followers should not stop with the circumcision but rather finish the job:

> Galatians 5:11-12 *And I, brethren, if I yet preach*
> *circumcision, why do I yet suffer persecution? then is the*
> *offence of the cross ceased. 12 I would they were even cut off*
> *which trouble you.*

As a matter of fact, this is the way verse 12 above is translated in the Contemporary English Version:

> 12 *I wish that everyone who is upsetting you would not*
> *only get circumcised, but would cut off much more!*

Furthermore, Jesus was scourged or whipped (Matthew 27:26) and was made to wear a crown of thorns (Matthew 27:29) which would have rendered him unacceptable as any kind of a sacrifice.

Some might say that the term "unblemished" means that the sacrifice was to be spiritually perfect, without sin. However, all animals are sinless, and do not have the capacity to sin against God. The term, "unblemished," must therefore refer to a physical perfection that, for Jesus, would have been ruined by scourging and by wearing a crown of thorns.

Christians believe that Jesus, who was a male, was their sin sacrifice of a lamb. However, we cannot find a passage in the Torah where God demands a male lamb to be sacrificed for sins.

If one wanted to offer a lamb for a sin sacrifice, it have to be female:

> Leviticus 4:32: *And if he bring a lamb for a sin offering, he shall bring it a female without blemish.*

Jesus was not a female, much less a female lamb. So Jesus could not be a sin offering.

Jesus could not have been a blood sacrifice for a sin committed in ignorance by the common person:

> Leviticus 4:27-28 *And if any one of the common people sin through ignorance, while he doeth somewhat against any of the commandments of the Eternal concerning things which ought not to be done, and be guilty; 28 Or if his sin, which he hath sinned, come to his knowledge: then he shall bring his offering, a kid of the goats, a female without blemish, for his sin which he hath sinned.*

He would have to have been both female, and a goat, but he was male and a human.

If Jesus was a sacrifice for sin through ignorance or an unwitting sin, he should not have been called the "lamb of God," but rather he should have been called "the goat of God" and have been female, since God specifies that the sin offering must be a female goat.

Jesus also could not have been a sacrifice for an inadvertently broken oath:

> Leviticus 5:4-6 *Or if a soul swear, pronouncing with his lips to do evil, or to do good, whatsoever it be that a man shall pronounce with an oath, and it be hid from him;*

when he knoweth of it, then he shall be guilty in one of these. 5 And it shall be, when he shall be guilty in one of these things, that he shall confess that he hath sinned in that thing: 6 And he shall bring his trespass offering unto the Eternal for his sin which he hath sinned, a female from the flock, a lamb or a kid of the goats, for a sin offering; and the priest shall make an atonement for him concerning his sin.

Once again, the sin sacrifice had to have been a "female from the flock, a lamb or goat."

Quite simply, Jesus would have been rejected by God even if he, as a human or just the human part of him, could have been offered as a sin sacrifice. There is no place in the Bible where a sin offering is supposed to be made of a male lamb. Jesus was not a lamb and he was not a female, he was a human being and male.

Chapter 9

The Messiah

Jews and Christians both use the term, "Messiah," but what each faith means by the term are two totally different concepts, they are mutually exclusive, and one cannot believe in them both at the same time. However, please remember that the Jews came first. The term, "Messiah," was first a Jewish concept before there were Christians. In fact, the word Messiah comes from the Hebrew term, "MaSHiaCH," meaning 'one who has been anointed,' and Hebrew is the ancient language spoken by the Jewish people. The concept of the Messiah involves a Jewish man who comes to the Jewish people and makes visible and tangible changes in the real world. These changes were defined by the Jewish people, based on the Jewish interpretation of the Jewish Bible. The term "Messiah," is a wholly Jewish term, reflecting a Jewish concept. No one has the right to change the meaning of a word coined and used by a people, as we learn from the following story:

Electricians Do Not Fix the Plumbing

A man named Jack was sitting at home reading a book when the lights suddenly went out on one side of his house. Of course, the first thing Jack did was check the breaker box outside, but he found nothing wrong. So, Jack went to his neighbors and asked if they knew a good electrician.

About an hour later, the doorbell rang. When Jack opened the door, he saw a man standing there with an arm full of pipes and wrenches.

"Hi! My name is Bill, and I am the electrician you called. I am here to fix your plumbing problem!"

Jack was surprised. He told the man, "You don't understand. I have an electrical problem, not a plumbing problem. My plumbing is fine. I need an electrician to fix the electricity in my home. Electricians do not fix the plumbing."

But it was too late. The man brushed by Jack, came into his home, and immediately started to fiddle with the plumbing. He tried to tighten the pipes in the kitchen, but they were fine. He tried to tighten the pipes in the bathroom, but there was nothing wrong with them, either. Every pipe he tried to fix did not need repair. So he left.

As soon as the "electrician" left, all of Jack's neighbors came over to his house. They said to Jack, "Wasn't Bill a great electrician?"

Jack responded, "He wasn't an electrician. Electricians do not fix the plumbing. He tried to fix the plumbing, but found that there was nothing wrong with the pipes. They haven't been changed one little bit since Bill was here. Nothing has been changed, I am still without electricity! What was broken before he came remains broken!"

However, Jack's neighbors insisted that Bill was a great electrician. "Oh, don't worry about the electrical problem, Jack. Bill will come back someday to prove to you that he was the electrician you were waiting for, and then he will fix the electricity. But until that day, you must believe that he was a great electrician!"

Jack had this same conversation with each of his neighbors. Finally, they began to tell him, "You know, Jack, you are the one with the problem. You must have a veil over your mind that prevents you from seeing the truth. You think that an electrician is supposed to fix the electricity, but that is not true. You have the wrong definition of the word 'electrician.' The real purpose of an electrician is to fix the plumbing. Someday, Jack, you will see that he really was a great electrician!"

Jack insisted that electricians do not fix the plumbing. However, he could do nothing to convince his neighbors that the true definition of the word "electrician" is someone who fixes electrical problems. Jack could not convince anyone that Bill was no electrician.

Like the electrician in the above story, Jesus came and went, and nothing in the world changed as a result, except the founding of a religion. Although we Jews created the term, "messiah," we are told by Christians that we have the wrong definition. What the Christians expected from their messiah, Jesus, is what they claim we Jews should have been expecting all along, just as Jack's neighbors thought that Jack should have expected that an electrician would fix the plumbing. In the same way that Bill "the electrician" came and went and the problems in Jack's house remained, so did Jesus come and go and the problems in the world also remain even until today.

These problems are the very same problems that Jews have always understood that the real messiah will fix when he comes. Our Christian neighbors may tell us that Jesus was the Messiah, like Jack's neighbors told him that Bill was a great electrician, but our definition, the original definition to the term "messiah," has not been fulfilled at all. We still wait for the real messiah, just as Jack, sitting in the dark, still must be waiting for a real electrician. Just as Jack's neighbors told him that Bill would return in a Second Coming, to do those things that Jack expected him to do the first time around, so do Christians tell Jews that Jesus will return in a Second Coming to do all those things the Real Messiah would have done the first time around.

The problem then, is deciding what a messiah is and who decides?

If there are two groups, and each one has a different definition of the same word, which group has the correct definition? Perhaps if the two groups created the term independently of each other and at the same time, one could say they both have a right to their own definition. But we Jews came first. The term "messiah" is our word, and no one has the right to come along and tell us our definition is wrong. For those who came after to tell us that our word now has the wrong meaning would be like someone who cannot speak English telling a native English speaking person that electricians fix the plumbing.

As we learned, the word "messiah," from the Hebrew word "MaSHiaCH," means "anointed." To anoint something is to pour oil over it on behalf of God, thus ritually dedicating it to a specific purpose or task in the world. Hence, anything anointed is *a* messiah. In the Bible, many things and many people are anointed.

In Exodus 28:41, Aaron and the priests are anointed, which means they each become a messiah:

> *And thou shalt put them upon Aaron thy brother, and his sons with him; and shalt anoint them, and consecrate them, and sanctify them, that they may minister unto me in the priest's office.*

Altars to God were also anointed:

> Genesis 28:18 *And Jacob rose up early in the morning, and took the stone that he had put for his pillows, and set it up for a pillar, and poured oil upon the top of it.*

> Exodus 29:36 *And thou shalt offer every day a bullock for a sin offering for atonement: and thou shalt cleanse the altar, when thou hast made an atonement for it, and thou shalt anoint it, to sanctify it.*

The Tabernacle and the Ark of the Covenant, as well as all of the utensils used for them, were also anointed:

> Exodus 30:26-29 *And thou shalt anoint the tabernacle of the congregation therewith, and the ark of the testimony, 27 And the table and all his vessels, and the candlestick and his vessels, and the altar of incense, 28 And the altar of burnt offering with all his vessels, and the laver and his foot. 29 And thou shalt sanctify them, that they may be most holy: whatsoever toucheth them shall be holy.*

> Exodus 40:9 *And thou shalt take the anointing oil, and anoint the tabernacle, and all that is therein, and shalt hallow it, and all the vessels thereof: and it shall be holy.*

Leviticus 8:10 *And Moses took the anointing oil,
and anointed the tabernacle and all that was therein, and
sanctified them.*

Matzah or unleavened bread, the priests, and kings were also
anointed:

Leviticus 2:4 *And if thou bring an oblation of a meat
offering baken in the oven, it shall be unleavened cakes of
fine flour mingled with oil, or unleavened wafers anointed
with oil.*

Exodus 30:30 *And thou shalt anoint Aaron and his
sons, and consecrate them, that they may minister unto me
in the priest's office.*

1 Samuel 15:1 *Samuel also said unto Saul, The
Eternal sent me to anoint thee to be king over his people,
over Israel: now therefore hearken thou unto the voice of the
words of the Eternal.*

1 Samuel 16:13 *Then Samuel took the horn of oil, and
anointed him in the midst of his brethren: and the Spirit
of the Eternal came upon David from that day forward. So
Samuel rose up, and went to Ramah.*

In the above examples, each thing or person anointed is *a*
messiah. However, when one uses the term, *The* Messiah, he is
using a term invented by the Jewish people. It is a Jewish concept
based on the Jewish interpretation of the Hebrew Scriptures, the
Jewish Bible, about a certain Jewish man who is to come to the Jews
and who makes real, visible, provable changes in the real world, the
world one sees outside of one's window. The Messiah is a title that
indicates a specific job, the job for which he has been anointed.

What, precisely, is the Christian definition to the word,
"messiah?" Christians believe that the messiah is someone who is

actually God, who is born as a human being on earth with a human being as a mother and God for a father, and who dies for the sins of humanity. To Christians, Jesus was the blood sacrifice they believe to be necessary for the forgiveness of sins. These sins are both those that we commit by our actions, but also the state of sinfulness that one is in, simply by being human. This state was passed down from one generation to the next and began with Adam and Eve when they sinned in the Garden of Eden.

For the above paragraph to be true, there is a lot more that one has to believe, above and beyond the simple statement that Jesus was the messiah. One has to believe that God became a human, or that a human can be God. One has to believe that one person can die for the sins of another. One has to believe that there needs to be a blood sacrifice for the forgiveness of sins. There is a whole theology behind the statement that Jesus was the messiah according to the Christian definition of the term. Other chapters of this book deal with each of these unbiblical beliefs.

You must understand that the Christian definition of the term, "messiah", has a greater connection to the beliefs that pagans in the ancient world had regarding their dying/saving man/gods. How do all Christians define the term messiah? They define it exactly as the pagans did some of their gods—they were born in the winter, died in the spring, and came back to life. It was believed that their followers would not die, but have immortal life, because the god's death acted as a sacrifice for the sins of the people. The pagan world was also filled with gods who were the product of a human mother and a god for a father. As we have seen elsewhere in this book, Hercules' mother was the human Alcmene, and his father was Zeus. Dionysus' mother was the human Semele, and his father, too, was Zeus.

When the earliest Christians came into the synagogues to proselytize, they were kicked out. They were not allowed to stay and preach; they were rejected because their message was pagan, was recognized as such by the Jews, and they were removed and separated from the Jewish people as a result. One can see that Jews recognized paganism in Christian theology in early Christian writings outside of their New Testament.

Justin Martyr (100-165) wrote a book called Dialogue With Trypho. Trypho was modeled on the Jews of Justin Martyr's day, and he put into Trypho's mouth Jewish objections to Christianity with which he was familiar. The sixty-seventh chapter of Dialogue with Trypho is titled, in part, "Trypho Compares Jesus With Perseus." Justin Martyr writes that Trypho objected to Christianity by saying, www.ccel.org/ccel/schaff/anf01.viii.iv.lxvii.html.

"'Moreover, in the fables of those who are called Greeks, it is written that Perseus was begotten of Danae, who was a virgin; he who was called among them Zeus having descended on her in the form of a golden shower. And you ought to feel ashamed when you make assertions similar to theirs, and rather [should] say that this Jesus was born man of men. And if you prove from the Scriptures that He is the Christ, and that on account of having led a life conformed to the law, and perfect, He deserved the honour of being elected to be Christ, [it is well]; but do not venture to tell monstrous phenomena, lest you be convicted of talking foolishly like the Greeks.'"

The early Jewish comparison of Christian theology to that of Perseus is also found in the writings of Origen (184-254), in his work, Contra Celsum, chapter 67.

(See http://www.ccel.org/ccel/schaff/anf04.vi.ix.i.lxviii.html)

This recognition of the comparison between Christianity and paganism, more than anything, is what caused the split between Judaism and Christianity, and between Jews and Christians.

Furthermore, the things that Christians claim Jesus did are not provable and can only be accepted on faith. For example, they claim that Jesus was born in Bethlehem, but there is no birth certificate. They claim that Jesus saves everyone from the tortures of a hell, but what is the proof? They say that Jesus performed miracles, and they further claim that the gospels are eyewitness accounts. All that they claim Jesus did must be taken on faith. Does this mean that the eyewitness accounts of the Koran, the Vedas of Hinduism, and the writings about the Buddha must also be believed? All those things that Christians claim Jesus did are not provable, but as we shall see below, all the things the real messiah will do according to Judaism will be provable and perceivable in the real world.

Who is the Messiah Supposed to be, and What Will He Do When He Gets Here?

First of all, the Jews have always defined the Messiah as someone who will be totally human, born of two human parents. But Jesus, according to Christian theology, was born of a union between a human woman and God, rather than of two human parents. This is seen in the book of Matthew:

> Matthew 1:18 *Now the birth of Jesus Christ was on this wise: When as his mother Mary was espoused to Joseph, before they came together, she was found with child of the Holy Ghost.*

The real Messiah is a direct, bloodline descendant of King David. Just as someone who is not from the proper bloodline cannot become the King of England, someone who is not from the proper bloodline cannot be the Messiah. Having a king for a father entitles one to inherit the throne. Currently, Prince Charles is next in line to inherit the throne and become King of England. If he gives up the throne, his brother Andrew does not inherit the throne. Instead, Charles' firstborn son William inherits the throne. Because David was a king, the lineage of kingship is promised only to his direct descendants. This means that the Messiah must be a direct descendant of King David. King David had many sons, one of whom was Solomon, who became King of Israel after King David. Therefore, the Messiah must also be a direct descendant of King David through King Solomon.

> Isaiah 11:1-10 *And there shall come forth a rod out of the stem of Jesse, and a Branch shall grow out of his roots: 2 And the spirit of the Eternal shall rest upon him, the spirit of wisdom and understanding, the spirit of counsel and might, the spirit of knowledge and of the fear of the Eternal; 3 And shall make him of quick understanding in the fear of the Eternal: and he shall not judge after the sight*

*of his eyes, neither reprove after the hearing of his ears: 4
But with righteousness shall he judge the poor, and reprove
with equity for the meek of the earth: and he shall smite
the earth with the rod of his mouth, and with the breath of
his lips shall he slay the wicked. 5 And righteousness shall
be the girdle of his loins, and faithfulness the girdle of his
reins. 6 The wolf also shall dwell with the lamb, and the
leopard shall lie down with the kid; and the calf and the
young lion and the fatling together; and a little child shall
lead them. 7 And the cow and the bear shall feed; their
young ones shall lie down together: and the lion shall eat
straw like the ox. 8 And the sucking child shall play on the
hole of the asp, and the weaned child shall put his hand
on the cockatrice' den. 9 They shall not hurt nor destroy
in all my holy mountain: for the earth shall be full of the
knowledge of the Eternal, as the waters cover the sea. 10
And in that day there shall be a root of Jesse, which shall
stand for an ensign of the people; to it shall the Gentiles
seek: and his rest shall be glorious.*

In the above quotation, David is the branch out of the roots, and the stem out of the rod of Jesse who was King David's father. The rod is David and the stem is the Messiah. In the last two lines, the "root of Jesse" refers to the Messiah. These verses also indicate some of the specific things that will happen when the Messiah comes. Humans will become vegetarians and all violence on the earth will stop. The phrase "for all the earth shall be full of the knowledge of the Eternal" means that all humans will become monotheists, and accept the Jewish God, the only God, as their God. However, these things have yet to happen. Just as the electrician did not repair the problems in Jack's home, Jesus did not change the problems that exist in the real world. All of the problems that existed before him still exist today. He did nothing to fulfill what it means to be the Messiah, which Christians admit when they invented the need for Jesus to return in a Second Coming.

Other quotations that explain that the Messiah must be a direct descendant of David are found in the following verses:

Jeremiah 23:5 *Behold, the days come, saith the Eternal, that I will raise unto David a righteous Branch, and a King shall reign and prosper, and shall execute judgment and justice in the earth.*

Ezekiel 34:23-25 *And I will set up one shepherd over them, and he shall feed them, even my servant David; he shall feed them, and he shall be their shepherd. 24 And I the Eternal will be their God, and my servant David a prince among them; I the Eternal have spoken it. 25 And I will make with them a covenant of peace, and will cause the evil beasts to cease out of the land: and they shall dwell safely in the wilderness, and sleep in the woods.*

Ezekiel 37:25 *And they shall dwell in the land that I have given unto Jacob my servant, wherein your fathers have dwelt; and they shall dwell therein, even they, and their children, and their children's children for ever: and my servant David shall be their prince for ever.*

Jeremiah 30:9 *But they shall serve the Eternal their God, and David their king, whom I will raise up unto them.*

Jeremiah 33:14-15 *Behold, the days come, saith the Eternal, that I will perform that good thing which I have promised unto the house of Israel and to the house of Judah. 15 In those days, and at that time, will I cause the Branch of righteousness to grow up unto David; and he shall execute judgment and righteousness in the land.*

Hosea 3:4-5 *For the children of Israel shall abide many days without a king, and without a prince, and without a*

*sacrifice, and without an image, and without an ephod,
and without teraphim: 5 Afterward shall the children of
Israel return, and seek the Eternal their God, and David
their king; and shall fear the Eternal and his goodness in
the latter days.*

Each quotation above speaks of the time when God will establish His Messiah, and in every instance it is a descendant of David who will reign.

But Jesus' lineage cannot go through his human father, according to Christian theology, as Jesus' father was not Joseph the husband of Mary. According to Christian theology, Jesus' father was God.

The Real Messiah Must Be a Direct Bloodline Descendant from King David, Only Through King David's Son Solomon, And Cannot Be Adopted Into the Davidic Line

In Judaism, one's lineage is inherited through one's father, so, traditionally; one is called up to the Torah for an aliyah by one's father's name. The idea that lineage is traced through one's father goes back to the Book of Numbers in the Torah, when God told the Israelites to take a census, and to count only through the fathers:

Numbers 1:2 *Take ye the sum of all the congregation
of the children of Israel, after their families, by the house of
their fathers, with the number of their names, every male
by their polls*

The Messiah also must be able to trace his lineage through his human father. According to Christian theology, God is Jesus' father, which means that Jesus cannot trace his lineage through a human father back through King Solomon to King David. Matthew and Luke both trace Jesus' lineage to Joseph, the husband of Mary. However, they insist that God, not Joseph, was Jesus' father. If Joseph was not the biological father, then his lineage is irrelevant because Jesus is not his bloodline descendant. Some argue, however, that Jesus was adopted by Joseph. Even if this is true, Jesus still could not be the Messiah because the Bible states that the Messiah must come forth from the body of David:

> 2 Samuel 7:12-17 *And when thy days be fulfilled, and thou shalt sleep with thy fathers, I will set up thy seed after thee, which shall proceed out of thy body; and I will establish his kingdom. 13 He shall build an house for my name, and I will establish the throne of his kingdom forever. 14 I will be his father, and he shall be my son. If he commit iniquity, I will chasten him with the rod of men, and with the stripes of the children of men: 15 But my mercy shall not depart away from him, as I took it from Saul, whom I put away before thee. 16 And thine house and thy kingdom shall be established forever before thee: thy throne shall be established forever. 17 According to all these words, and according to all this vision, so did Nathan speak unto David.*

The following quote provides additional evidence that the Messiah must be a direct descendant of Solomon:

> 1 Chronicles 22:9-10 *Behold, a son shall be born to thee, who shall be a man of rest; and I will give him rest from all his enemies round about: for his name shall be Solomon, and I will give peace and quietness unto Israel in his days. 10 He shall build an house for my name; and he shall be my son, and I will be his father; and I will establish the throne of his kingdom over Israel forever.*

In spite of the above, let us pretend for a moment that the lineage of Joseph could be used as the lineage of Jesus. As it was discussed earlier, the lineage of the Messiah must be traced to King David through his son Solomon. However, the Gospel of Luke traces Joseph's lineage back to King David through his son Nathan,

Solomon's step-brother, as you can read in the verse below from Luke. This would be like someone presently claiming the throne of England because he is a descendant of Andrew, the brother of Prince Charles, when the throne can only go through Prince Charles and his descendants. This provides yet another reason that Jesus cannot be the Messiah, should Christians cling to their claim that his lineage can be traced through Joseph:

> Luke 3:31-32 *Which was the son of Melea, which was the son of Menan, which was the son of Mattatha, which was the son of Nathan, which was the son of David, 32 Which was the son of Jesse, which was the son of Obed, which was the son of Boaz, which was the son of Salmon, which was the son of Naasson,*

The Real Messiah Cannot Be a Descendant of Jehoiakim, or Jeconiah, or Shealtiel

Certain people were cut off from being inheritors to the throne of King David. Jehoiakim so angered God that God declared that none of his descendants can sit on the throne of King David and rule over Judah which the real messiah will do. The following verses show that the descendants of Jehoiakim include Shealtiel:

> 1 Chronicles 3:15-17 *And the sons of Josiah were, the firstborn Johanan, the second Jehoiakim, the third Zedekiah, the fourth Shallum. 16 And the sons of Jehoiakim: Jeconiah his son, Zedekiah his son. 17 And the sons of Jeconiah; Assir, Shealtiel his son,*

Several other verses refer to the curse placed on these specific descendants. In the following example, God tells others not to feel sorry for Jehoiakim because he is to be cursed:

> Jeremiah 22:18 *Therefore thus saith the Eternal concerning Jehoiakim the son of Josiah king of Judah; They shall not lament for him, saying, Ah my brother! or, Ah sister! they shall not lament for him, saying, Ah Eternal! or, Ah his glory!*

God also declares that all of Jehoiakim's descendants are cursed, regardless of their individual worth:

> Jeremiah 22:24 *As I live, saith the Eternal, though Coniah the son of Jehoiakim king of Judah were the signet upon my right hand, yet would I pluck thee thence;*

The following verse provides the actual curse placed on Jehoiakim by God:

> Jeremiah 22:30 *Thus saith the Eternal, Write ye this man as childless, a man that shall not prosper in his days: for no man of his seed shall prosper, sitting upon the throne of David and ruling any more in Judah.*

The curse on Jehoiakim is significant because, according to Matthew 1:11-12 and Luke 3:27, Jesus is a descendant of this cursed man through Shealtiel. Both books of the New Testament explain that Jesus is a descendant of Shealtiel, who is the grandson of Jehoiakim. The curse placed on Jehoiakim also applies to Jesus, his descendant through Shealtiel, the son of Jeconiah who was the son of Jehoiakim, meaning that he cannot be the Messiah:

> Matthew 1:11-12 *And Josias begat Jechonias and his brethren, about the time they were carried away to Babylon: 12 And after they were brought to Babylon, Jechonias begat Shealtiel; and Shealtiel begat Zorobabel;*

> Luke 3:27 *Which was the son of Joanna, which was the son of Rhesa, which was the son of Zorobabel, which was the son of Shealtiel, which was the son of Neri,*

Christianity knew there was a problem with the lineage of Jesus from the beginning. This is why Paul tells the early Christians to disregard the problems with Jesus' genealogies when he wrote:

> 1 Timothy 1:4 *Neither give heed to fables and endless genealogies, which minister questions, rather than Godly edifying which is in faith: so do.*

> Titus 3:9 *But avoid foolish questions, and genealogies, and contentions, and strivings about the law; for they are unprofitable and vain.*

Some might claim that the curse on Jehoiakim was lifted because a descendant of his became the governor of Judea. However, the text of the curse states that his descendants will not sit on the throne of David. The curse means that they will never have complete sovereignty over the Promised Land. As only a governor, appointed by a government other than his own, no descendant of Jehoiakim ever had sovereignty, just as the curse promised.

What is the Job for Which the Messiah was Anointed?

The real Messiah will make changes in the real world, changes that one can see, perceive, and prove. It is for this task that the real Messiah has been anointed in the first place, hence the term, messiah—one who is anointed. These changes that one will be able to see and perceive in the real world include the following:

1. Heralding the Messiah, and with the same goals as the Messiah, Elijah appears

The Messiah has a specific job description, which the Bible explains in detail. Elijah the prophet, who will herald the coming of the Messiah, has the same goals as the Messiah. The following verse explains that both Elijah and the Messiah will bring families closer together:

> Malachi 4:5-6 *Behold, I will send you Elijah the prophet before the coming of the great and dreadful day of the Eternal: 6 And he shall turn the heart of the fathers to the children, and the heart of the children to their fathers, lest I come and smite the earth with a curse.*

In Matthew 10:34-37, however, Jesus says he comes not to bring peace, but to turn families against one another so that their foes will be the people of their own household:

> *34 Think not that I am come to send peace on earth: I came not to send peace, but a sword. 35 For I am come to set a man against his father, and the daughter against her mother, and the daughter in law against her mother in law. 36 And a man's foes shall be they of his own household. 37 He that loveth father or mother more than me is not worthy of me: and he that loveth son or daughter more than me is not worthy of me.*

Furthermore, Malachi above tells us that Elijah returns, preceding the coming of the Messiah. Although Jesus claimed that John the Baptist was Elijah ("Elias" in our translation), John the Baptist did not know that he was Elijah instead:

> Matthew 11:12-14 *And from the days of John the Baptist until now the kingdom of heaven suffereth violence, and the violent take it by force. 13 For all the prophets and*

> *the law prophesied until John. 14 And if ye will receive it, this is Elias, which was for to come.*

> John 1:19-21 *And this is the record of John, when the Jews sent priests and Levites from Jerusalem to ask him, Who art thou? 20 And he confessed, and denied not; but confessed, I am not the Christ. 21 And they asked him, What then? Art thou Elias? And he saith, I am not. Art thou that prophet? And he answered, No.*

It is also interesting to note that even though John the Baptist had baptized Jesus, instantly recognizing Jesus as the messiah, 8 chapters later, still in Matthew, John the Baptist was unsure. In Matthew 3:13-15, John was reluctant to baptize Jesus because he recognized who he was:

> *Then cometh Jesus from Galilee to Jordan unto John, to be baptized of him. 14 But John forbad him, saying, I have need to be baptized of thee, and comest thou to me? 15 And Jesus answering said unto him, Suffer it to be so now: for thus it becometh us to fulfil all righteousness. Then he suffered him.*

But in Matthew 11:2-3, John must have forgotten that he had earlier recognized Jesus as the expected messiah:

> *Now when John had heard in the prison the works of Christ, he sent two of his disciples, 3 And said unto him, Art thou he that should come, or do we look for another?*

2. King David's dynasty is reestablished through the Messiah's own children, who reign over all the earth

In order to reestablish King David's dynasty and to allow that dynasty to carry on, the Messiah will have children who will rule after his death.

Daniel 7:13-14 *I saw in the night visions, and, behold, one like the son of man came with the clouds of heaven, and came to the Ancient Of Days, and they brought him near before him. 14 And there was given to him dominion, and glory, and a kingdom, that all people, nations, and languages should serve him his dominion is an everlasting dominion, which shall not pass away, and his kingdom that which shall not be destroyed.*

However, Jesus had no children through which this dynasty can be reestablished.

3. There is peace between all nations, between all peoples, and between all individuals

The following verses demonstrate the ways in which the Messiah will bring peace. There will be no war and all weapons will be destroyed.

Isaiah 2:2-4 *And it shall come to pass in the last days, that the mountain of the Eternal's house shall be established in the top of the mountains, and shall be exalted above the hills; and all nations shall flow unto it. 3 And many people shall go and say, Come ye, and let us go up to the mountain of the Eternal, to the house of the God of Jacob; and he will teach us of his ways, and we will walk in his paths: for out of Zion shall go forth the law, and the word of the Eternal from Jerusalem. 4 And he shall judge among the nations, and shall rebuke many people: and they shall beat their swords into plowshares, and their spears into pruninghooks: nation shall not lift up sword against nation, neither shall they learn war any more.*

Micah 4:1-4 *But in the last days it shall come to pass, that the mountain of the house of the Eternal shall be established in the top of the mountains, and it shall be exalted above the hills; and people shall flow unto it. 2 And many nations shall come, and say, Come, and let us go up to the mountain of the Eternal, and to the house of the God of Jacob; and he will teach us of his ways, and we will walk in his paths: for the law shall go forth of Zion, and the word of the Eternal from Jerusalem. 3 And he shall judge among many people, and rebuke strong nations afar off; and they shall beat their swords into plowshares, and their spears into pruninghooks: nation shall not lift up a sword against nation, neither shall they learn war any more. 4 But they shall sit every man under his vine and under his fig tree; and none shall make them afraid: for the mouth of the Eternal of hosts hath spoken it.*

Ezekiel 39:9 *And they that dwell in the cities of Israel shall go forth, and shall set on fire and burn the weapons, both the shields and the bucklers, the bows and the arrows, and the handstaves, and the spears, and they shall burn them with fire seven years.*

Obviously, world peace is not yet a reality. Furthermore, Jesus said in Matthew 10:34 (referenced earlier), that his purpose in coming was to bring a sword, and not peace. Of all the things that Jews have longed for over the millennia, peace is paramount and is prayed for, often, within the traditional Jewish prayer book. Since there is no peace, and since Jesus said he never intended to bring peace, Jesus was clearly not the messiah.

4. The world becomes vegetarian

If violence cannot exist, meat eating cannot exist, because to kill the animal requires violence to be done against it in taking its life and to slaughter it. Therefore, all human beings and animals will become vegetarians as we read in Isaiah:

Isaiah 11:6-9 *The wolf also shall dwell with the lamb, and the leopard shall lie down with the kid; and the calf and the young lion and the fatling together; and a little child shall lead them. 7 And the cow and the bear shall feed; their young ones shall lie down together: and the lion shall eat straw like the ox. 8 And the sucking child shall play on the hole of the asp, and the weaned child shall put his hand on the cockatrice' den. 9 They shall not hurt nor destroy in all my holy mountain: for the earth shall be full of the knowledge of the Eternal, as the waters cover the sea.*

5. All weapons of war are destroyed

All weapons of war will be destroyed, either to be burned in a fire or to be buried:

Ezekiel 39:9 *And they that dwell in the cities of Israel shall go forth, and shall set on fire and burn the weapons, both the shields and the bucklers, the bows and the arrows, and the handstaves, and the spears, and they shall burn them with fire seven years:*

Ezekiel 39:12 *And seven months shall the house of Israel be burying of them, that they may cleanse the land.*

6. The gentiles come to Judaism, or at least to monotheism

When the messiah comes, God will establish a new covenant with the Jews that will differ from the previous one. The existing covenant requires that people look to the Bible to learn what God wants from them. The new covenant will exist within people's hearts so that all they must do is look within themselves. God will already have planted there what he wants from people. Furthermore, missionizing will be unnecessary because all people will inherently know God.

The following verses are commonly quoted by Christian missionaries because they refer to a "new covenant," and this is discussed at length in Part II of this book.

> Jeremiah 31:31-34 *Behold, the days come, saith the Eternal, that I will make a new covenant with the house of Israel, and with the house of Judah. 32 Not according to the covenant that I made with their fathers in the day that I took them by the hand to bring them out of the land of Egypt; which my covenant they broke, although I was an husband unto them, saith the Eternal. 33 But this shall be the covenant that I will make with the house of Israel; After those days, saith the Eternal, I will put my law in their inward parts, and write it in their hearts; and will be their God, and they shall be my people. 34 And they shall teach no more every man his neighbor, and every man his brother, saying, Know the Eternal: for they shall all know me, from the least of them unto the greatest of them, saith the Eternal: for I will forgive their iniquity, and I will remember their sin no more.*

Many Christians believe the above verses are a prophecy of the Christian New Testament. However, if the new covenant already exists today, Christians would no longer need to missionize, and people would not have to read the Bible (or any other book) because they would already know what God wants from them. It is obvious that the covenant described in these verses has not yet been made. The new covenant will be made with the Jews, not the gentiles. Through the Jews, all other people will learn what God wants from them. As long as people have to missionize others to their beliefs, the new covenant has not been made.

7. There is universal recognition that the Jewish idea of God is God

The book of Isaiah contains the same basic idea that the world will become fully Jewish or, at least, fully monotheistic.

> Isaiah 11:9 *They shall not hurt nor destroy in all my holy mountain: for the earth shall be full of the knowledge of the Eternal, as the waters cover the sea.*

In the same way that the bottom of the sea is covered by water, the knowledge of God covers all people all over the earth.

> Zechariah 14:9 *And the Eternal shall be king over all the earth: in that day shall there be one Eternal, and his name one.*

The following quotation refers to the Jewish holiday of Sukkot, the feast of tabernacles. This provides an explanation of why some Christians celebrate Sukkot today. According to the Bible, when the Messiah comes, the entire world will celebrate this holiday. Because Christians believe that the Messiah has already come in Jesus, some celebrate this Jewish holy day.

> Zechariah 14:16 *And it shall come to pass, that every one that is left of all the nations which came against Jerusalem shall even go up from year to year to worship the King, the Eternal of hosts, and to keep the feast of tabernacles.*

8. The Jews are sought for spiritual guidance

After the Messiah arrives, all nations of the earth will look to the Jews for advice.

Zechariah 8:23 *Thus saith the Eternal of hosts; In those days it shall come to pass, that ten men shall take hold out of all languages of the nations, even shall take hold of the skirt of him that is a Jew, saying, We will go with you: for we have heard that God is with you.*

9. There is an end to all forms of idolatry

Zechariah 13:2 *And it shall come to pass in that day, saith the Eternal of hosts, that I will cut off the names of the idols out of the land, and they shall no more be remembered: and also I will cause the prophets and the unclean spirit to pass out of the land.*

However, the world remains steeped in idolatry.

10. There Is an Ingathering of The Twelve Tribes

The Messiah will also take the Jews from the scattered parts of the world and bring them into their land, the Promised Land given to them by God, the Land of Israel.

Ezekiel 36:24 *For I will take you from among the heathen, and gather you out of all countries, and will bring you into your own land.*

Isaiah 43:5-6 *Fear not: for I am with thee: I will bring thy seed from the east, and gather thee from the west: 6 I will say to the north, Give up; and to the south, Keep not back: bring my sons from far, and my daughters from the ends of the earth;*

However, many of the ten tribes remain lost, and not all Jews live in Israel.

11. The Temple is rebuilt

The Temple, first built by King Solomon, destroyed by the Babylonians, rebuilt under Cyrus of Persia, but again destroyed by the Romans, will be rebuilt:

> Isaiah 2:2 *And it shall come to pass in the last days, that the mountain of the Eternal's house shall be established in the top of the mountains, and shall be exalted above the hills; and all nations shall flow unto it.*

> Ezekiel 37:26-28 *Moreover I will make a covenant of peace with them; it shall be an everlasting covenant with them: and I will place them, and multiply them, and will set my sanctuary in the midst of them for evermore. 27 My tabernacle also shall be with them: yea, I will be their God, and they shall be my people. 28 And the heathen shall know that I the Eternal do sanctify Israel, when my sanctuary shall be in the midst of them for evermore.*

However, the temple has yet to be rebuilt.

12. Famine ceases to exist

> Ezekiel 36:29-30 *I will also save you from all your uncleannesses: and I will call for the corn, and will increase it, and lay no famine upon you. 30 And I will multiply the fruit of the tree, and the increase of the field, that ye shall receive no more reproach of famine among the heathen.*

However, people continue to starve to death each day.

13. Death ceases to exist

At some point after the Messiah comes, death will stop occurring and there will be a final judgment of all people.

> Isaiah 25:8 *He will swallow up death in victory; and the Eternal God will wipe away tears from off all faces; and the rebuke of his people shall he take away from off all the earth: for the Eternal hath spoken it.*

However, people continue to die each day.

14. The dead are resurrected

The prophet Isaiah knows that resurrection of the dead will not take place during his own life, but he explains that dead men (including him) will one day live again.

> Isaiah 26:19 *Thy dead men shall live, together with my dead body shall they arise. Awake and sing, ye that dwell in dust: for thy dew is as the dew of herbs, and the earth shall cast out the dead.*

In the following quote, Daniel speaks of a final judgment that, according to Judaism, does not refer to hell. The shame and contempt to which he refers does not mean eternal suffering and torture. For example, Adolf Hitler is a name thought of with everlasting contempt. He does not suffer eternal torture, but his name, his image, his life, is the epitome of what other human beings should not do.

> Daniel 12:2 *And many of them that sleep in the dust of the earth shall awake, some to everlasting life, and some to shame and everlasting contempt.*

Ezekiel 37:12-13 *Therefore prophesy and say unto them, Thus saith the Eternal God; Behold, O my people, I will open your graves, and cause you to come up out of your graves, and bring you into the land of Israel. 13 And ye shall know that I am the Eternal, when I have opened your graves, O my people, and brought you up out of your graves*

Isaiah 43:5-6 *Fear not: for I am with thee: I will bring thy seed from the east, and gather thee from the west; 6 I will say to the north, Give up; and to the south, Keep not back: bring my sons from far, and my daughters from the ends of the earth;*

15. All other nations help the Jews materially

When the messiah comes, the nations of the earth give to the Jews their wealth, much as the Egyptians gave of their wealth to the Hebrew slaves at the Exodus.

Isaiah 60:5-6 *Then thou shalt see, and flow together, and thine heart shall fear, and be enlarged; because the abundance of the sea shall be converted unto thee, the forces of the Gentiles shall come unto thee. 6 The multitude of camels shall cover thee, the dromedaries of Midian and Ephah; all they from Sheba shall come: they shall bring gold and incense; and they shall show forth the praises of the Eternal.*

Isaiah 60:10-12 *And the sons of strangers shall build up thy walls, and their kings shall minister unto thee: for in my wrath I smote thee, but in my favour have I had mercy on thee. 11 Therefore thy gates shall be open continually; they shall not be shut day nor night; that men may bring unto thee the forces of the Gentiles, and that their kings may be brought. 12 For the nation and kingdom that will not serve thee shall perish; yea, those nations shall be utterly wasted.*

Isaiah 61:6 *But ye shall be named the Priests of the Eternal: men shall call you the Ministers of our God: ye shall eat the riches of the Gentiles, and in their glory shall ye boast yourselves.*

16. The Jewish People are characterized by eternal gladness and joy

Isaiah 51:11 *Therefore the redeemed of the Eternal shall return, and come with singing unto Zion; and everlasting joy shall be upon their head: they shall obtain gladness and joy; and sorrow and mourning shall flee away.*

17. The Egyptian river runs dry

Isaiah 11:15 *And the Eternal shall utterly destroy the tongue of the Egyptian sea; and with his mighty wind shall he shake his hand over the river, and shall smite it in the seven streams, and make men go over dryshod.*

18. Trees yield their fruit monthly in Israel

Ezekiel 47:12 *And by the river upon the bank thereof, on this side and on that side, shall grow all trees for meat, whose leaf shall not fade, neither shall the fruit thereof be consumed: it shall bring forth new fruit according to his months, because their waters they issued out of the sanctuary: and the fruit thereof shall be for meat, and the leaf thereof for medicine.*

19. Each Tribe of Israel receives its inheritance

Each tribe will go back to that part of the Promised Land that was promised to them and to their ancestors.

> Ezekiel 47:13-14 *Thus saith the Eternal God; This shall be the border, whereby ye shall inherit the land according to the twelve tribes of Israel: Joseph shall have two portions. 14 And ye shall inherit it, one as well as another: concerning that which I lifted up mine hand to give it unto your fathers: and this land shall fall unto you for inheritance.*

20. All nations on earth will acknowledge their sins against the Jews

The nations of the earth will recognize that they have been wrong, that the Jews have been right, and that the sins of the Gentile nations, their persecutions and the murders of Jews which they committed, have been borne by the Jewish people. This is shown in the very famous passage of Isaiah 53, and is discussed, at length, in Part II of this book.

These are most of the things that make up the job description of the Messiah, for which he will be anointed, those things which are to happen when the Messiah comes. None of these things has occurred yet, which means the Messiah has not yet come. Even Christians recognize that none of the above has happened yet. This is why Christianity invented the idea of a Second Coming. The real Messiah has no need to come a second time to do the things he was supposed to do the first time. The real Messiah will accomplish these tasks in his own lifetime.

Keep in mind the story at the beginning of this chapter. The electrician came into Jack's home, changed absolutely nothing, and then left. The Jews created the term Messiah, and the Jews defined the term. As we said above, for anyone else to come to the Jews and say that this definition is incorrect, and that the Messiah must die for our sins (an unbiblical concept), is like someone who does not speak English saying that an electrician is a person who repairs plumbing.

Chapter 10

THE DEFINITION OF A JEW

Many people, Christians and some Jews as well, erroneously believe that just as one can be Black and Christian, just as one can be Asian and Christian, one can also be Jewish and Christian. This belief is not true because the Jews are not a race. There is no genetic code passed from either mother or father to the child that makes that child a Jew. Recent discoveries of common genetic codes found in Jews only show that a person's ancestors most likely were Jewish, but this does not make that person a Jew. Although one cannot convert to become a member of a race (one cannot convert to become an Asian or Black), one who converts to Judaism does become fully a Jew.

The fact that one who was not born a Jew can become a Jew by converting to Judaism can be seen in the Bible. In the Book of Esther, we are told that many Persians became Jews:

> Esther 8:17 *And in every province, and in every city, whithersoever the king's commandment and his decree came, the Jews had joy and gladness, a feast and a good day. And many of the people of the land became Jews; for the fear of the Jews fell upon them.*

Some might believe that to truly be a Jew, one had to be a member of the tribe of Judah, since the English word "Jew" is derived from the word "Judah." But the Book of Esther dispels this myth as well. The Book of Esther calls Mordechai, who was from the tribe of Benjamin, a Jew:

Esther 2:5 *Now in Shushan the palace there was a certain Jew, whose name was Mordechai, the son of Jair, the son of Shimei, the son of Kish, a Benjamite.*

The Bible is clear, one need not be from the tribe of Judah to be called a Jew, and one can convert to Judaism and become a Jew. Similarly, if one converts from Judaism to another faith, one is no longer a Jew.

When the non-Jewish world makes the claim that someone who was Jewish but converts to Christianity can retain "Jewish culture and ethnicity," one must ask, "Which Jewish culture? Which Jewish ethnicity?" The culture and ethnicity of a Jew from Morocco has little in common with the ethnicity and culture of a Jew from Eastern Europe. Yet, both are Jews because their faith—their Judaism—is the same.

If follows that just as many people convert to Judaism and become Jews, those who convert out of Judaism are no longer Jews. The Biblical basis for this is I Kings 18:21. Elijah the prophet addresses the Jews who were beginning to slip into the worship of Baal.

I Kings 18:21 *And Elijah came unto all the people, and said, How long halt ye between two opinions? If the Lord be God, follow him: but if Baal, then follow him. And the people answered him not a word.*

Elijah's point is that the people must choose one or the other, because they cannot simultaneously believe in two opposite, mutually exclusive ideas. Judaism and Christianity believe in opposite, mutually exclusive ideas. You cannot be a Jew and believe that Jesus was the Messiah at the same time (see Chapter 9 regarding the Messiah). There are those who were born Jews but who have accepted Jesus. They may wish to believe that they are still Jewish and they may call Jesus by what they think was his Hebrew name, they may call themselves by Hebrew names to make what they have done sound more Jewish, but they have, in fact, left Judaism and the Jewish people.

The Jews determine who is a Jew, and not ex-Jews who have converted to Christianity, or Christians who are wannabees-Jews. Jewish law is clear on this issue, as one can see in the Responsa, the legal decisions made by rabbis over the last two millennia.

A Rabbi in the later Middle Ages named the Hai Gaon, as quoted by Aderet in Responsa VII #292, stated that a Jew who converted out of the faith was no longer a Jew. This belief was shared by numerous rabbis and can be seen in the Responsa literature of Simon ben Zemah of Duran, Samuel de Medina, Judah Berab, Jacob Berab, Moses ben Elias Kapsali, and others in the Middle Ages. Moses Isserles demanded a formal conversion back to Judaism for those who converted out of Judaism, but who then wanted to return to Judaism. He demanded ritual immersion (mikveh) and repentance before a court of three (beit din). This is also seen in other Responsa literature, including Radbaz, Responsa III, 415; Moses Isserles to Yoreh Deah 268.12; and Hoffman, Melamed Leho-il II, 84.

Most recently, this can also be seen in the Responsa of the Satmar Rov in his Divrei Torah, Yoreh Deah #59, paragraph 5, as well as in the Responsa of Rabbi Moshe Feinstein, Even Haezer Volume 4 Number 53.

Moses ben Maimon, called Maimonides, also wrote that if a Jew converts to Christianity, he or she is no longer a Jew. See Maimonides, Hilchot Mamrim Perek 3, Halacha 1-3, as well as Maimonides' Mishnah Torah, Avodat Kochavim 2:5.

It was only after the experience of the Conversos, Jews who were forced by the church to convert to Catholicism but who secretly practiced Judaism (Crypto-Jews), that the rabbis stated that one who converted involuntarily out of Judaism did not have to convert back to Judaism. This assumes that because the conversion was forced, the Jew in his heart never really left the Jewish religion. This also concerns only those who wish to return to Judaism. It says nothing about those who accept the theology of Christianity as their own and therefore remain Christian.

This concept is not applicable to the case of anyone else, anywhere else, who converts to Christianity today. In the modern world, no one is given the three choices of leaving the country of their birth, death, or conversion to Christianity, as the Jews of Europe were given by Christians in the Middle Ages. It was the fact that they were forced to convert which gave reason to this leniency.

Modern Israel has a law called the Law of Return, which deals with this very issue. The law states that because Israel is the Jewish homeland, one who is Jewish and can prove it can come to Israel and immediately become an Israeli citizen, as one who is coming home.

Daniel Rufeisen was born Jewish, of two Jewish parents. Because of the Nazi persecutions, he fled from his home. Eventually, on his own volition, he chose to convert to Catholicism and eventually became a priest. Father Daniel, aware of his parents' heritage, once having belonged to a Zionist youth organization, and having saved about 100 Jews during the Holocaust, came to Israel and applied to become a citizen of Israel under the Law of Return. The Israeli Supreme Court denied his application, stating that because he converted, he was no longer a Jew. He had to wait the customary time for any other non-Jew to become a naturalized Israeli citizen. This is similar to the situation in the United States, where one must wait years to become a naturalized citizen.

Please note that as a Jew, Father Daniel was lost, one more success for the Nazis.

More recently, the same thing happened to a Messianic "Jewish" couple. The Beresfords from South Africa tried to become citizens of Israel under the Law of Return, using the justification that their parents were Jewish. They were denied on the same basis as Father Daniel. Remember that all of the parents involved, the parents of Daniel Rufeisen, and the parents of both of the Beresfords, were Jews. Furthermore, it is interesting to note that the man leading the fight against the Beresfords for the Israeli Department of Immigration was an Orthodox rabbi and member of the Orthodox Israeli political party known as Shas. As an Orthodox rabbi, he would have been well versed in Jewish law on this subject.

This rabbi's attitude is held by many Orthodox rabbis today. Orthodox Rabbi Aryeh Kaplan, writing for the Union of Orthodox Jewish Congregations of America, for the National Conference of

Synagogue Youth (the Orthodox Youth Group), in his book The Real Messiah, on page 11, wrote the following:

"This brings us back to our original question: What can a Jew lose by embracing Christianity?

The answer is: Everything.

Christianity negates the fundamentals of Jewish faith, and one who accepts it rejects the very essence of Judaism. Even if he continues to keep all of the rituals, it is the same as if he abandoned Judaism completely.

A Jew who accepts Christianity might call himself a 'Jewish Christian,' but he is no longer a Jew. He can no longer even be counted as part of a Jewish Congregation."

As an act of leniency, however, few rabbis today ask the ex-Jew returning to Judaism to go through all of the rituals for conversion. This might be a "stumbling block before the blind," before those who wish to return. So long as one remains a Christian, one is no longer a Jew. But if one wishes to return to Judaism, the return is made easier as an act of compassion.

Similarly, as long as one believes that Jesus was anything more than a human being who lived and died around 2,000 years ago, that person cannot convert to Judaism, and become a Jew. The two faiths of Judaism and Christianity are simply mutually exclusive and incompatible.

This topic leads to other questions, including:

Are the majority of Jews who are secular, many not believing in God at all, really Jews?

Yes, just as a U.S. citizen is still a citizen even if they never vote, even if they do not celebrate July Fourth, or even not have turkey on Thanksgiving, they are still U.S. citizens. But if they become a citizen of another country, especially another country that is hostile to America, they lose their U.S. citizenship, even if they were to continue to celebrate July Fourth and have turkey on the American Thanksgiving. Similarly, if a person converts to Judaism, they become a Jew, and if one converts out of Judaism, they are no longer a Jew, even if they were to keep kosher and keep the Sabbath like real Jews.

This is how a Jew is defined: A Jew is a member of a nation defined by the religion of Judaism. Let me explain:

I am not talking about a nation meaning a country (like the State of Israel), which is defined by borders and passports. Rather, I am talking about a nation in the same sense we understand it in relationship to the Native American Indians. For them, we used to use the term "tribe," but the term "nation" is more accurate. For the Jews, the analogy to a nation is a perfect analogy, because that, indeed, is what God told Abraham God would make Abraham into:

Genesis 12:2 *And I will make of you a great nation . . .*

God did not promise Abraham that He would make of him a great culture, or a great ethnic group. We are a nation, a nation defined by our religion, because it is in the religious literature of our religion—the Bible—that tells us that we are a nation.

For a person to become a citizen of a nation, they must go through a process called naturalization. To become a "citizen of the Jewish nation," to become a Jew, the naturalization process is called conversion to the religion of Judaism. The process is actually quite similar. To become a citizen of the United States, one studies the law, learns about our country, and learns the customs and celebrations of the American People. This is what one does when converting to Judaism. One learns Jewish law, learns about Israel, and learns the customs and celebrations of Judaism, the faith of the Jewish People.

This is another reason why we are defined by our religion, because it is the religious conversion to the religion that makes one a member of the nation. On the other hand, just because a Jew does not practice the religion of Judaism, it does not mean that he or she is no longer a citizen, no longer a Jew, unless that person converts to another religion.

This can be explained by taking a look at four analogies:

1. Andy is born in the U.S. of two U.S. citizens, but Andy moves to Australia. There, he remains involved in every U.S. election, he knows every issue relating to his home city, his home county, his home state, and even on the federal level. He writes his congressional leaders, he has turkey on the fourth Thursday in November, and celebrates July Fourth with fireworks.

   Even though he lives in Australia, does Andy remain a U.S. citizen? Yes, he remains a U.S. citizen because he has done nothing to give up his citizenship.

   Similarly, there are those Jews who actively pursue being Jewish, who affiliate with the Jewish People by joining synagogues, by becoming active in Jewish organizations, who celebrate the holidays and holy days, life cycle events, etc.

2. Bert is born in the U.S. of two U.S. citizens, but he moves to Belgium. There, Bert cannot care less about anything about or from the U.S. As long as Bert has a job, food, and television, he is quite content. Bert cannot remember who is President of the United States, much less what any issues there might be. He does not even realize that the fourth Thursday in November means anything, and he does not remember the significance of July Fourth.

   Even though Bert lives in Belgium and does nothing to participate as a U.S. citizen, to express or promote the values of democracy, etc., does Bert remain a U.S. citizen? Yes, he remains a U.S. citizen because he also has done nothing to lose his U.S. citizenship.

   Similarly, there are those Jews who do nothing Jewishly, who do not affiliate with any synagogue or temple or Jewish organization, who do not keep the commandments, who do not celebrate Jewish holidays or holy days or observe the Sabbath. However, they remain, nevertheless, Jews, until such time as they convert to another religion.

3. Charlie is born in the U.S. of two U.S. citizens, but Charlie moves to China. There, Charlie does everything possible to overthrow the U.S. government. Charlie puts on sackcloth and ashes every July Fourth, and ignores Thanksgiving. Charlie attempts to smuggle arms into the U.S. and overthrow the government, and works to fight everything for which it stands.

Even though Charlie lives in China and works to destroy the U.S., does Charlie remain a U.S. Citizen? Yes, because working to overthrow the U.S. government does not constitute grounds for losing one's citizenship. Those who oppose the U.S. in this way simply are tried in court and go to jail.

There are those Jews whose actions could be, and are, detrimental and destructive to Judaism and to the Jewish People. Nevertheless, these people remain Jews.

The only time that Andy, Bert, or Charlie would ever lose their U.S. citizenship is if, and when, they accepted the citizenship of another country—an act that usually renounces one's U.S. citizenship. Of course, the U.S. recognizes dual citizenship in some instances with certain other countries, but Judaism and the Jewish nation do not recognize dual citizenship at all. The act of accepting another faith removes a person from "citizenship" in the Jewish "nation." A Jew who has accepted the theology of another faith is no longer a Jew according to Jewish law as we discussed above.

Now, we come to Danny.

4. Danny is born in the U.S. of a father who is a U.S. citizen, but Danny's mother is Dutch. At the age of 18, Danny must choose between Dutch and U.S. citizenship. But Danny cannot choose Brazilian citizenship because he was not born there, and because he has no connection to Brazil through his mother or through his father. According to international

and U.S. laws, Danny can obtain the rights for citizenship to countries through either his mother or father.

According to Jewish law, citizenship rights in the Jewish nation only come through the mother, while inheritance rights, which are related to lineage, come through the father. An example of the latter might be inheriting property or being a member of a specific tribe, like that of Benjamin, or Levi, which come through the father. Now, in the past couple of decades, only the Reform movement of Judaism has accepted the "citizenship" rights of those Jews whose lineage comes through their father. This is done only in cases where the child was raised with specific and exclusively Jewish ceremonies and affiliations (a fact usually not stated, but nevertheless true).

As a Jew, one has been chosen by God to act as God's advertising agent in the world. God needs Jews to be a constant reminder to the rest of the world that God exists, and that God demands moral and ethical behavior from God's creation. What it means to be Jewish, now that we have defined it, is to have a mission in the world. That mission, as defined by our covenant with God, is to be a light unto the nations, through our actions and through our invitation to all others to join us in our mission by becoming Jews. Those actions are not merely ethical behavior on our part—they are the commandments that are intended to make us different and holy (the word "holy" means "different") through our observance of them.

If one joins any other faith, as Messianic "Jews" have done by accepting Jesus as their personal savior and Messiah, they are no longer Jews. They are Christians. This also includes the New Agers as well as the once Jewish Buddhists. They have joined a religion that is Wholly Other to Judaism. To simply deny an element of a faith is very different from joining another faith, being baptized into it, etc. Those messianic "Jews" want to see themselves as still Jewish, even though they now believe exactly the same as the members of the Southern Baptist, Lutheran Church—Missouri Synod, and Assemblies of God churches. It is these churches and denominations that fund, establish, and maintain messianic "synagogues."

This leads to two questions that one might wish to ask those who have become Messianic "Jews."

First of all, if these groups are still Jewish, then why is it that the people who fund them are not their "fellow" Jews? These organizations that are intent on making Jews into Messianic "Jews" do not receive any funds from the Jewish Federations, or from other Jewish organizations like the Anti-defamation League (the ADL), or the American Jewish Committee, or any other Jewish organization. As a matter of fact, these Jewish organizations release statements condemning these fake Jewish organizations intent on proselytizing Jews and turning them into Christians. Many of these Jewish organizations have committees whose purpose is to combat these fake Jewish organizations.

Another question one might wish to ask of Messianic "Jews" is whether or not they believe that a Jew who does not believe in Jesus is going to hell? As Good Christians, they have chosen a faith that does, in fact, believe that the Jews who do not accept Jesus are, indeed, going to go to hell. This would mean that as soon as a person becomes Christian, as soon as they accept Jesus as their personal savior, son of God, and Messiah, they then condemn those who are supposedly in their own group. Real Jews do not condemn other Jews to an eternity of torture in Hell for not believing in Jesus. Talk about trying to have one's cake and eat it too! This means that the Messianic "Jews" condemn to hell the very group of which they still claim to be a part. Does this make sense?

To the Jewish community, it is ridiculous to claim one can be a Jew and a Christian at the same time, and knowledgeable Jews are not fooled.

CHAPTER 11

THE "JEWISH ROOTS" OF CHRISTIANITY

The newest technique in convincing Jews to convert to Christianity is to make the Jewish targets believe that they are not leaving Judaism by converting to Christianity, that one can be a Jew and a Christian at the same time. The way in which this is accomplished is to couch Christian beliefs in Jewish practices, to give to Jewish rituals a Christian spin, so that the targets can continue to appear and to act Jewishly, but what they are doing is understood through Christian theological interpretations.

This technique is justified by Christian missionaries' interpretation of I Corinthians 9:20-22, where they claim Paul states that it is acceptable for missionaries to pretend to be anything, as long as it gets converts to Christianity:

> *20 And unto the Jews I became as a Jew, that I might gain the Jews; to them that are under the law, as under the law, that I might gain them that are under the law; 21 To them that are without law, as without law, (being not without law to God, but under the law to Christ,) that I might gain them that are without law. 22 To the weak became I as weak, that I might gain the weak: I am made all things to all men, that I might by all means save some.*

Christian missionaries also quote Philippians 1:18 to justify pretending to be Jews, which expresses a similar idea:

> What then? Notwithstanding, every way, whether in
> pretence, or in truth, Christ is preached; and I therein do
> rejoice, yea, and will rejoice.

According to the interpretation of Christian missionaries, Paul in I Corinthians 9:20-22 justifies deceptive practices, and in Philippians 1:18 he distinguishes between pretense and truth. He then condones both in the service of proselytizing others to Christianity.

This is most often seen in the practices of those known as Messianic "Jews." Erroneously those who follow this form of Christianity may be called "Jews for Jesus," but this confuses the name of a mission to the Jews with those Jews who have succumbed to its proselytizing and to that of other such Christian organizations who exist only to missionize Jews to Christianity.

Were you to compare the theology of the Jews for Jesus organization and that of Messianic "Jews" with the theology of the Southern Baptist Convention (SBC), you would see no difference. Compare the statements of faith of the Messianic Jewish Alliance of America (whose original name was the Hebrew Christian Alliance of America), with the statement of faith from the SBC. They can both be found on the internet. Similarly, one could look at the websites for any Messianic "synagogue" and compare its statement of beliefs with those of the Southern Baptist Convention or any Baptist church, Assemblies of God church, or any other such church of any Christian denomination and see not just similarities but duplication, except the use of more Jewish-sounding words by the Messianic "Jews" to make it appear that what they believe remains Jewish.

This technique, that one can remain a Jew even when one accepts the theology of Christianity and becomes a Christian, is proposed in what Christians call "Indigenous Cultural Evangelism," which says that as long as a missionary makes the targets think they can be both a Christian and whatever they were before their conversion, then missionizing them will be easier. (See: Understanding Church Growth, by Donald A. McGavran, the section on The Sociological Foundation).

This is what is happening when Christians teach about something they call "The Jewish Roots of Christianity." One might think that the term, "Jewish Roots," refers to the Christian idea that Christianity developed from Judaism, that it is based on the Hebrew Scriptures, or that the first Christians were Jews. This is not what they mean.

A story:

David had a beautiful garden in which he grew perfect tomatoes. One day, his friend Matthew planted cucumbers right in the middle of the garden. When the cucumbers sprouted, Matthew claimed the tomatoes were the roots of his cucumbers. In other words, he said the cucumbers developed from the tomatoes and were the natural result—the goal—of the tomatoes as they grew to maturity.

The above story may seem ridiculous, but it accurately represents the claims of many people who teach the "Jewish roots of Christianity." They plant Christian cucumbers, so to speak, in the midst of Jewish tomatoes, and then claim that what they planted there sprouted naturally from what was already growing. In other words, they put a Christian theological interpretation into a Jewish ceremony or ritual. They then claim that this planted Christian theological interpretation, having been "found" in something Jewish (because it was planted there by them in the first place), proves the "Jewish Roots" of Christianity. This is nonsense, and shows the lengths to which many will go to obtain Jewish legitimacy, and to make it look like what these Christians are doing is Jewish.

Consider the following example. During the Jewish holiday of Passover, three pieces of matzah are placed on the Seder plate. During the Seder, the middle matzah is taken out, broken in two, and one of these two pieces (called the Afikomen) is then hidden, and brought out at the end of the meal. Some Christians will claim the matzah, as well as the ritual of the Afikomen, is symbolic of Jesus, and therefore indicates that the basic theology of Christianity can be found in Jewish rituals, and therefore indicate the "Jewish

Roots" of Christianity. They claim that the three pieces of matzah represent the Trinity—"the Father, Son, and Holy Spirit." Please take note that it is the middle matzah, the son in the Trinity, that is taken out and broken (crucified), hidden (buried), and brought back out (resurrected). The matzah used today also has stripes and lines of holes. To these same Christians, the stripes and holes also indicate the "Jewish roots" of Christianity, because the stripes and holes represent the marks on Jesus from the scourging he received, and the holes represent those on Jesus that were caused by the crucifixion.

The problem with this explanation is that it is absolutely untrue. There was no Seder, no Haggadah, no three pieces of Matzah on any Seder plate, and no Seder plate, at the time of Jesus. The ritual to observe the Jewish Holiday of Passover, especially as we know the ritual today, developed hundreds of years after Jesus died. In addition, the first discussions of a Passover ritual describe only one and one half of a piece of matzah. Originally, the half-piece was broken in half, and one of these two pieces, now one-fourth of the original matzah, was set aside to be eaten as the last part of the meal. It was not hidden; it was merely set aside, remaining in plain view. The idea of hiding the Afikomen originated in the middle 1600s in Germany as a way to keep children interested in the service, and the idea eventually caught on throughout the Jewish world. The matzah of today has stripes and holes because it is machine made. The machine causes the stripes and the holes as it pulls the dough through it. This machine was invented only about 150 years ago, in the mid 1800s. It could not be a foreshadowing of the death of Jesus, because it developed long after Jesus died. One thing cannot foreshadow something that came before it. That the matzah represents Jesus is only a Christian interpretation.

Of course, Christian missionaries and those who want to believe that Christianity originated from Judaism can interpret anything in a Christian way. This does not mean Christianity developed from the things they are interpreting. If this were the case, the same logic could be applied to pizza.

Pizza has three basic elements: bread, tomato sauce, and cheese. The middle element is the tomato sauce, which is red. One could easily provide a Christian base for these three definitive elements of pizza by saying the three basic ingredients of pizza represent the Trinity.

The bread

Jesus calls himself the bread of life in John 6:35:

> And Jesus said unto them, I am the bread of life: he that cometh to me shall never hunger; and he that believeth on me shall never thirst.

Pizza dough must be kneaded, and this image of kneading the dough parallels the beating Jesus received prior to his crucifixion. The pizza dough is then rolled over with an instrument, which pokes holes in it to remove any air. This parallels Jesus' receiving the holes in is body from the crucifixion, just like they claim is represented in the matzah.

The tomato sauce

The sauce is red like Jesus' blood, and it is spread on the dough in the same way the blood of a sacrifice is placed on an altar.

The cheese

The cheese covers the rest of the pizza like the death of Jesus covers the sins of the people.

This explanation demonstrates how anything, even pizza, can be used to symbolize Jesus. However, does this mean the symbolism found in pizza proves "The Pizza Roots of Christianity?" Of course not.

A Christian might ask, "But weren't the first Christians actually Jews?" Yes, but this is irrelevant. The first Protestants were Roman Catholics, and Martin Luther was a Roman Catholic priest. However, Roman Catholics do not consider Protestant Christianity to be merely another form of Roman Catholicism or the goal of Roman Catholicism, nor do they consider Protestants to be Completed Roman Catholics, as Christians insultingly call ex-Jews who have become Christians "completed Jews."

The Apocryphal book of I Maccabees explains that the first person killed in the Maccabee's rebellion was a Jew. He was killed because of his willingness to sacrifice a pig to Zeus, which Mattathias had earlier refused to do. Obviously, this Jew must have been very secular and assimilated. Had he survived Mattathias's attack against him and later formed a religion dedicated to the worship of Zeus and Zeus's half-human sons, would that make his newly formed faith just another form of Judaism? If he called this newly formed faith, "Jews for Zeus," or "Jews for Zeus' Half-Human Sons," would this make it a faith with "Jewish Roots?" Certainly not! Just because one is a Jew, it does not mean that everything he or she does or believes is Jewish.

There are no Jewish roots of Christianity. The theology that supports it, and from which it is derived, is antithetical to what the Bible says. It is diametrically the opposite of what Judaism believes, and it has far more in common with the pagan idolatry of the Hellenist and Roman dying/saving man/gods than with anything in the Hebrew Scriptures, except where Christians wish to give the Hebrew Scriptures their Christian interpretation and spin. This leads us to Part II of this book.

PART II

A CONTRAST IN THE INTERPRETATION OF THE HEBREW SCRIPTURES

Chapter 12

Introduction to Interpretation

1. The reader is always convinced that the Bible says what the reader means

Everyone has beliefs and experiences and attitudes that influence one's thinking, and which influence the way in which one understands what he or she sees and hears. This is especially true when it comes to religion, and even more so when one reads the Bible. Someone reading a passage with a Christian viewpoint will understand that passage in a totally different way than one who is Jewish. When it comes to understanding the Bible, there is an old saying that "the reader is always convinced that the Bible says what the reader means." In other words, the reader sees reflected in the Bible what his or her experiences and beliefs lead him or her to see there, and not necessarily what is inherently a part of the Biblical verse, or what the Biblical verse is literally saying.

Truly, everyone is free to take any single verse in the Bible, or even a paragraph in the Bible, and interpret it in any way he or she wishes to interpret it. Since the only thing one person can say about another person's interpretation is that he or she does or does not agree with that interpretation, then to some extent, all interpretations are equal, and equally valid or equally invalid, depending on one's religious perspective. When it comes to the interpretation of a single verse of Scripture, there can be no objectively true way to understand it, as all interpretations are subjective. This is what makes them interpretations.

Judaism and Christianity both hold beliefs that are mutually exclusive to the other. For example, one cannot believe, as Christians do, that Jesus died for their sins, while at the same time holding the belief, as Jews do, that no one else can die for your sins. How, then, can one determine which of the two beliefs is True? The only way to do so is to compare the beliefs of both faiths to what the Bible states, literally and with no interpretation, as we have done in Chapter 6. It would further help if one can see a pattern of the same belief, a consistency of belief, either throughout the Bible or in at least one or two other places within the Bible.

There are reasonable, well-reasoned Christian interpretations of Scripture, but from the Jewish perspective, those interpretations must be rejected as simply wrong, because they go against the meaning, against both the literal meaning as well as against the way in which Jews have interpreted the Biblical text for thousands of years.

In response to the Christian belief that Jesus died for their sins, the Jews will point out no less than three places in the Bible that contradict this idea, as discussed in Chapter 6 of this book. In Exodus 32:30-35, Deuteronomy 24:16, and Ezekiel 18:20 it is clear, only the one who sinned is the one who gets the punishment, each person dies for his own sin, and the wickedness of the wicked is upon the wicked, not upon someone else who is righteous. These verses are clear, they are consistent throughout the entire Bible, and they need no interpretation to understand. For those who believe in the Bible, one must therefore reject the Christian understanding that Jesus died for their sins.

By comparing the way in which Christianity has interpreted a verse or a collection of verses in the Bible to other verses in the Bible, we can test whether or not the interpretation Christians have given is truly what the Bible is saying, or whether it is simply their interpretation of a verse based on the already existing beliefs of the Christian reader. Furthermore, when Jews come to understand the Jewish argument regarding the proper interpretation of a Biblical verse, the Christian interpretation loses its validity and reasonableness.

2. That is what makes you a Christian and me a Jew

To a great extent, what a person sees in a particular Biblical verse tells us more about that person than it tells us about that Biblical verse. The way in which a person has chosen to interpret a Biblical verse is what makes that person a Jew or a Christian, as much as being a Jew or being a Christian will determine how one interprets a Biblical verse. For the Christian, it is not only that they read a verse from the Bible in a Christian way, it is also that their Christian faith leads them to interpret the Bible in a Christian way that makes them Christian. The same could be said about the Jew, that it is the Jew's Judaism that leads the Jew to interpret the Bible in a Jewish way.

Often, when it comes to Biblical interpretations, there will be an impasse, a stale-mate. The Jews will not understand or accept the interpretation of the Bible from a Christian perspective, nor will the Christian understand or accept the interpretation of the Bible from a Jewish perspective.

Moreover, if a Jew were to accept the Christian interpretation of a Biblical verse that goes against Jewish beliefs, it would be a step towards making that Jew into a Christian. If a Christian were to accept the Jewish interpretation of a Biblical verse that goes against Christian beliefs, it would be a step towards making that Christian into a Jew. Indeed, this is the way in which Christian missionaries have converted Jews to Christianity over the last two millenia. They introduce their targets to their way of understanding the Hebrew Scriptures that conforms to the Christian interpretation, and the Jew, for whatever reason, chooses to accept the Christian interpretation.

When a Jew and a Christian argue about the meaning of a particular verse, and reach an impasse, then it is simply good to acknowledge that the way in which one chooses to understand or interpret a Biblical verse is what makes that person who he or she is, just as who he or she is will determine how one chooses to interpret a Biblical verse.

3. **Veil over the Jewish mind Versus seeing the world through Christian-colored glasses**

Christians believe that the Jews are blinded by a veil that covers our minds, preventing us from seeing the relationship between the Biblical verses of the Hebrew Scriptures and Jesus. Paul, in the Christian's New Testament writes:

> 2 Corinthians 3:13-16 *13 And not as Moses, which put a veil over his face, that the children of Israel could not steadfastly look to the end of that which is abolished: 14 But their minds were blinded: for until this day remaineth the same veil untaken away in the reading of the old testament; which veil is done away in Christ. 15 But even unto this day, when Moses is read, the veil is upon their heart. 16 Nevertheless when it shall turn to the Lord, the veil shall be taken away.*

In other words, Jews have a veil covering their minds that keeps them blind to the supposed truth of Christianity found in the Jews' own Hebrew Scriptures, which is only removed when they become a Christian.

However, this statement admits that the Christian interpretation is only that, an interpretation, and is not an inherent, literal understanding of the Biblical text. If the veil is only "done away in Christ," if one has to become a Christian to see a verse's relationship to Jesus, then the prophecy of Jesus or the verse's relationship to Jesus is not an inherent, literal, obvious meaning found in the text. Otherwise, one would not have to be a Christian to see it there, it would be obvious to any reader. By stating that the veil is only "done away in Christ," or that only when one "turns to the Lord" is the veil "taken away," Christians are admitting that their understanding of the Bible can only be seen if viewed through the lens of Christianity.

Rather than a veil in front of the minds of Jews which blinds us to the "truth" of Christianity, the Christians are reading the Hebrew

Scriptures through Christian-colored glasses, or the Christian meaning would be obviously evident to a Jew or Christian or Muslim or Atheist who reads it, even if he or she then were to reject its message. This means that the Christian interpretation of the Bible is simply and only that, an interpretation, and from the Jewish perspective, it is wrong, because it is only their interpretation, and it does not reflect what the verse states and what one reads elsewhere in the Bible.

4. Ownership of the text

Every faith's sacred texts have verses that are very subject to interpretation. Each faith has the right, because the texts are theirs, to explain and to interpret their texts to an outsider, who might find those texts to be objectionable. The outsider may choose to reject that faith's interpretation, but each faith has a right to understand its own Scriptures in its own way.

For example, in the Christian's New Testament, we read in the Gospel of Luke where Jesus said:

> Luke 14:26 *If any man come to me, and hate not his father, and mother, and wife, and children, and brethren, and sisters, yea, and his own life also, he cannot be my disciple.*

The verse from Luke clearly and literally states that in order to be a disciple of Jesus, one must hate one's family. Also found in Matthew is a statement that Jesus made that indicates his purpose in coming was to alienate families from each other, introduced by a verse that states that Jesus' purpose in coming was not to bring peace, but rather to bring a sword:

> Matthew 10:34-37 *Think not that I am come to send peace on earth: I came not to send peace, but a sword. 35 For I am come to set a man at variance against his father,*

and the daughter against her mother, and the daughter in law against her mother in law. 36 And a man's foes shall be they of his own household. 37 He that loveth father or mother more than me is not worthy of me: and he that loveth son or daughter more than me is not worthy of me.

These verses are not in keeping with what Judaism expects in a Messiah. Christians, of course, have the right to explain their Testament's verses through their own interpretations, and the Jews have the right to reject the Christian interpretation. However, if Christians have the right to explain their Testament's verses, so do the Jews have a right to explain their Testament's verses, and the Christians have the right to reject the Jewish understanding of the Biblical text.

It must be said, however, that, obviously, Judaism came before Christianity, and therefore the greater burden is on the Christian to prove that the Christian interpretation of the Jewish Scriptures is true and should replace the Jewish interpretation. This leads us to the next chapter, where we will look at the techniques used by Christianity to interpret the Bible.

CHAPTER 13

TECHNIQUES OF CHRISTIAN INTERPRETATION

Christians use five techniques of interpretation, and examples of each are found in their own New Testament. They are:

A. Mistranslations

Christians can base the interpretation on a mistranslation, or mistranslate a verse to fit an already existing belief. However, the true and accurate translation of the original Hebrew indicates that the verse cannot properly be understood in the way Christians interpret it.

B. Out of Context

Christians take a verse out of the context in which it is found in the Hebrew Scriptures to make it look like Jesus fulfilled that one verse. However, when one reads that verse in the context in which it was originally found, it cannot be properly understood in the way Christians interpret it.

C. Inventions

Christians can invent a verse that does not actually exist in the Hebrew Scriptures, and then invent a story about Jesus to show that he fulfilled this non-existent verse. Christians can also invent a story about Jesus to show that Jesus fulfilled a prophecy found in the Hebrew Scriptures.

D. Typologies

Christians can interpret a story of a character in the Hebrew Scriptures to be what they call a type, or model, of Jesus, making what is found in the Hebrew Scriptures a prophecy in and of itself. This form of interpretation differs from the others in that it uses as its basis, the character in a story, or the story itself, rather than a verse or verses.

E. Prooftexts

Christians can take a single verse or a few verses from the Hebrew Scriptures and claim that the verse or verses are, in and of themselves, a prophecy of the coming of the messiah which they believe that Jesus fulfilled. The verse or verses from the Hebrew Scriptures that they treat in this way are called prooftexts, because the verses or texts are used to prove that Jesus was the messiah. Indeed, the verse or verses become a prooftext for them when they use the techniques listed above, of Mistranslations, Out of Context, or Inventions. This technique will have its own chapter and we will look at the 10 most common verses used in this way by Christians in proselytizing Jews and the Jewish response.

A. Mistranslations

The fact that events in Jesus' life are based on mistranslations, or a verse in the Biblical text is mistranslated to reflect an already existing belief, can be seen from the following quotation from Matthew. In it, Matthew describes how the miraculous birth of Jesus from a virgin fulfils a Biblical prophecy:

> Matthew 1:18-25 *Now the birth of Jesus Christ was on this wise: When as his mother Mary was espoused to*

Joseph, before they came together, she was found with child of the Holy Ghost. 19 Then Joseph her husband, being a just man, and not willing to make her a public example, was minded to put her away privily. 20 But while he thought on these things, behold, the angel of the Lord appeared unto him in a dream, saying, Joseph, thou son of David, fear not to take unto thee Mary thy wife: for that which is conceived in her is of the Holy Ghost. 21 And she shall bring forth a son, and thou shalt call his name Jesus: for he shall save his people from their sins. 22 Now all this was done, that it might be fulfilled which was spoken of the Lord by the prophet, saying, 23 Behold, a virgin shall be with child, and shall bring forth a son, and they shall call his name Emmanuel, which being interpreted is, God with us. 24 Then Joseph being raised from sleep did as the angel of the Lord had bidden him, and took unto him his wife: 25 And knew her not till she had brought forth her firstborn son: and he called his name Jesus.

This quotation from Matthew is based on a story found in Isaiah 7:1-16 which you can read below. The story in Isaiah is about Ahaz, King in Jerusalem over 700 years before the time of Jesus. Ahaz was terrified of two enemy kings who were marching on Jerusalem. Isaiah is sent to Ahaz to calm his nerves and to give Ahaz a sign that would prove that God was on Ahaz's side. When told to ask for a sign, out of fear, Ahaz refuses to test God by requesting a specific sign. Isaiah then names the sign that God would give to Ahaz. That sign is that a woman who was already pregnant would soon give birth to a male. Remember, a sign is not a miracle. A sign is something real, that points to something else, just like a stop sign is real metal and real paint, and points to the place in the road where one is to stop. The child himself is the sign, and his conception was not meant or referred to by Isaiah to be anything special or miraculous. Isaiah calls the son a sign, and not a miracle. As a sign, every time Ahaz would see the child, he would be comforted to know that God was on his side, and that he had nothing to worry about from those enemy kings. That is what made the child a sign to Ahaz. This is also why the son's name was to be "EmanuEl," which means "God Is With Us." Every time Ahaz had to call the child by name, he would be reminding himself that "God is with us," and not with Ahaz's enemies.

Isaiah tells Ahaz that by the time that child was old enough to be able to tell the difference between Good and Evil, the two enemy kings would be dead. How old is a child before he or she is old enough to know the difference between Good and Evil? Some might say by the age of two or three. Others may claim around the age of 12 or 13, the ages of a Bat or Bar Mitzvah. This means that the sign was meant for Ahaz's own time as the first verse below states, and not for a time that was 700 years in Ahaz's future:

> Isaiah 7:1-16 *And it came to pass in the days of Ahaz the son of Jotham, the son of Uzziah, king of Judah, that Rezin the king of Syria, and Pekah the son of Remaliah, King of Israel, went up toward Jerusalem to war against it, but could not prevail against it. 2 And it was told the house of David, saying, Syria is confederate with Ephraim. And his heart was moved, and the heart of his people, as the trees of the wood are moved with the wind. 3 Then said the Eternal unto Isaiah, Go forth now to meet Ahaz, thou, and Shear-yashuv thy son, at the end of the conduit of the upper pool in the highway of the fuller's field; 4 And say unto him, Take heed, and be quiet; fear not, neither be fainthearted for the two tails of these smoking firebrands, for the fierce anger of Rezin with Syria, and of the son of Remaliah. 5 Because Syria, Ephraim, and the son of Remaliah, have taken evil counsel against thee, saying, 6 Let us go up against Judah, and vex it, and let us make a breach therein for us, and set a king in the midst of it, even the son of Tabeal: 7 Thus saith the Eternal God, It shall not stand, neither shall it come to pass. 8 For the head of Syria is Damascus, and the head of Damascus is Rezin; and within threescore and five years shall Ephraim be broken, that it*

be not a people. 9 And the head of Ephraim is Samaria,
and the head of Samaria is Remaliah's son. If ye will not
believe, surely ye shall not be established. 10 Moreover the
Eternal spoke again unto Ahaz, saying, 11 Ask thee a sign
of the Eternal thy God; ask it either in the depth, or in the
height above. 12 But Ahaz said, I will not ask, neither will
I tempt the Eternal. 13 And he said, Hear ye now, O house
of David; Is it a small thing for you to weary men, but will
ye weary my God also? 14 Therefore the Eternal himself
shall give you a sign; Behold, the young woman (ha-almah)
has conceived (harah) and shall bear a son, and shall call
his name Immanuel. 15 Butter and honey shall he eat, that
he may know to refuse the evil, and choose the good. 16 For
before the child shall know to refuse the evil, and choose the
good, the land that thou abhorrest shall be forsaken of both
her kings.

The word which is mistranslated is the word for "the young woman" (in Hebrew: ha-almah). The fact that she is called "the young woman," and the definite article, "the" is used, indicates that the young woman was known to both Isaiah and to Ahaz and therefore must have lived in their day. The fact that this all took place in the time of Ahaz is further indicated by the past tense "has conceived (Harah)." One may argue that a young woman could also be a virgin, but the point is that the word does not refer to her sexual status. Had the Biblical Author wished to express the idea that the woman was a virgin, the Author would have used the Hebrew word for virgin, which is "b'tu-lah." Even if the text had called her a virgin, there is no reason to believe that the virgin would have conceived her child through any other means than through a sexual act. It is only reading the verse through the eyes of Christianity, assuming a virgin birth, that would lead one to interpret the verse in this way.

The fact that "almah" does not mean virgin can be shown by looking at the use of the same word in Proverbs 30:18-20. Here again the word "almah" is used in the Hebrew. However, here there is no question that the young woman is not a virgin. These verses are an expression of amazement that things can happen which leave no trace that they have occurred. These things include the fact that two people can make love and leave no trace that they have had sexual intercourse. This can only be true if the woman was not a virgin, because the loss of her virginity would be an indication that she had engaged in sex. We also know this because "the young woman" is likened to an adulterous woman who commits adultery through the act of sexual intercourse but leaves no trace of the transgression. This could only make sense because she, as an adulterous woman was not a virgin:

> Proverbs 30:18-20 *There are three things which are too wonderful for me, yea, four which I know not: 19 The way of an eagle in the air; the way of a serpent upon a rock; the way of a ship in the midst of the sea; and the way of a man with a young woman <almah>. 20 Likewise is the way of an adulterous woman; she eateth, and wipeth her mouth, and saith, I have done no wickedness.*

Christians might say that there is a dual prophecy regarding these verses, that one prophecy was fulfilled in the days of Isaiah and Ahaz, but another prophecy based on the same verse was fulfilled by Jesus. However, why claim that there is only a dual prophecy to this or to any other verse in Scripture? Perhaps there is a third or triple prophecy and the third prophecy was fulfilled by any of the many gods who were the product of a virgin birth, the result of a human woman being made pregnant by a god, but without the sexual act? Perhaps this was a triple prophecy, the third being fulfilled by Perseus, who was the son of the human woman named Danae and who had Zeus for a father? Zeus made Danae pregnant by showering her with gold rather than through the sexual act, which was like a virgin birth. Or maybe this could have been a quadruple prophecy or more. If one allows for a dual prophecy, there is no reason to say that the number would stop at two, except through the wishful thinking of Christian theology.

So we see that the whole story of the virgin birth is based on a mistranslation of the word "ha'almah." Therefore remember that when a Christian missionary, or missionary literature, references a verse from the Hebrew Scriptures, look up the verse in the original Hebrew. The Christian translation may be a mistranslation.

It is possible that the early Christians wanted to have the birth story of their Jesus to reflect the same miracle nature as the birth stories of the pagan gods of their day, and so they latched onto the mistranslation found in the Septuagint (Greek translation) of the verse from Isaiah and built their story of Jesus' birth upon this verse. It is not that the mistranslation of a Biblical verse led to the belief about Jesus, but rather that the belief in Jesus, that he had to be born of a virgin, for example, led to the use of a mistranslated verse to validate the already held belief.

The earliest Christians might have been Jews, but they were very assimilated into Hellenism and the culture of that time. Since other gods had miracle births, like that of Perseus explained above, it is possible that they first had the belief about the virgin birth of Jesus, and then found a verse that had already been mistranslated to use to indicate that Jesus was fulfilling that verse. The earliest Christians who were Jews used the Septuagint translation of the Hebrew Scriptures into Greek, far more often than the original Hebrew. This is another great indication of just how assimilated into Greek pagan culture these early Christianized Jews were.

The word "Septuagint" should only refer to the Greek translation of the Torah, the five books of Moses, and not to the whole of the Hebrew Scriptures. The word "Septuagint" comes from the Greek word for "seventy," a reference to the story of seventy Jewish scholars who translated the Torah into Greek in rooms separated from one another, but who came out with exactly the same translation. Later Greek translators took the remaining books of the Hebrew Scriptures, but we do not know who they were, and their translations are just not that accurate to the original Hebrew. Isaiah was translated by one of these unknown translators. Eventually, all of the books of the Jewish Bible were translated into Greek and collected together. Unfortunately, these translations are incorrectly collectively called the "Septuagint," but in truth, the term "Septuagint" really should only refer to the Greek translation of the Torah and not to the translation of the rest of the books of the Jewish Bible.

Whether these early Christians first had the belief that their Jesus was born of a virgin like so many other pagan gods and then found a passage in the Septuagint's mistranslation to justify their belief, or that they just based their story on the mistranslation of the word "ha-almah," cannot be known. What is known is that the basis of their interpretation remains an incorrectly translated Hebrew word.

B. Out of Context

The fact that stories in the life of Jesus are based on verses taken out of context can best be seen by examining the following story taken from Matthew 2:13-15. Matthew tells the story of Joseph and Mary taking Jesus to Egypt to flee from Herod who wanted to kill Jesus. When Herod died, Joseph and Mary returned to the Promised Land. According to the story in Matthew, taking Jesus out of Egypt was a supposed fulfillment of a verse found in one of the Prophets:

> Matthew 2:13-15 *And when they were departed, behold, the angel of the Lord appeareth to Joseph in a dream, saying, Arise, and take the young child and his mother, and flee into Egypt, and be thou there until I bring thee word: for Herod will seek the young child to destroy him. 14 When he arose, he took the young child and his mother by night, and departed into Egypt: 15 And was there until the death of Herod: that it might be fulfilled which was spoken of the Lord by the prophet, saying, 'Out of Egypt have I called my son.'*

The verse that Matthew claims was fulfilled by Jesus when he came out of Egypt is found in Hosea. But was God, in the Book of Hosea, referring to the messiah, to God's supposedly half-human son, or to someone else? Let us look now at the whole quotation found in Hosea 11:1:

> When Israel was a child, I loved him, and out of Egypt have I called my son.

Thus we see that Hosea was referring to Israel, the nation, as God's child whom He took out of Egypt. Hosea must be referring to something specific in order to call Israel the son of God. Hosea referred to the time when Israel was a child. This had to be the Exodus from Egypt, the event in Jewish history which began the history of Israel as a nation and not just as descendants of the Patriarchs. Hosea is referring to Exodus 4:21-23. In this passage, God is telling Moses what to say to Pharaoh, and God, Himself, refers to Israel as His son:

> 21 And the Eternal said unto Moses, When thou goest to return into Egypt, see that thou do all those wonders before Pharaoh, which I have put in thine hand: but I will harden his heart, that he shall not let the people go. 22 And thou shalt say unto Pharaoh, Thus saith the Eternal, Israel is my son, even my firstborn: 23 And I say unto thee, Let my son go, that he may serve me: and if thou refuse to let him go, behold, I will slay thy son, even thy firstborn.

Thus we see that Matthew ignored the fact that Hosea was referring explicitly to Israel in her youth as a nation. Matthew quoted only the second half of the verse from Hosea and he based his story of Jesus on this half of the verse.

This would be comparable to someone making the claim that King David was an atheist because in the Bible he stated, "There is no God." Indeed, the phrase is found in the Book of Psalms, written by King David. However, upon looking at the entire context of the phrase, one would read:

Psalm 51:1 *A Psalm of David. The fool hath said in his heart, There is no God.*

King David was not an atheist, and reading the entire verse one sees that he was calling atheists fools.

It is important to note that this story of Jesus going into and then out of Egypt appears only in Matthew. Even though Matthew takes the phrase, "and out of Egypt have I called my son," out of its original context, Matthew makes it look as though the story of Jesus fleeing to Egypt fulfills a Biblical prophecy. However, as noted above, Luke says nothing of Jesus ever going into Egypt. This would mean that if Matthew were right, and going into and then out of Egypt was some sort of Biblical prophecy, then according to Luke, Jesus never fulfilled it.

Therefore remember that when a Christian missionary, or missionary literature, makes a reference to a verse from the Hebrew Scriptures, look up the entire context in which it is found. In its entire context, it may not say, at all, what Christians portray it as saying.

C. Inventions

Inventions of Verses

The fact that Christians invented a verse that does not actually exist anywhere in the Hebrew Scriptures can be shown from Matthew 2:23. In this verse the author of Matthew makes it look as though the sentence, "He shall be called a Nazarene" is a verse from a prophet in the Hebrew Scriptures. As a matter of fact, there are Christian translations of their New Testament that put the entire sentence, "He shall be called a Nazarene" in quotation marks, to emphasize that it is, indeed, a verse quoted from the Hebrew Scriptures. However, there is no verse in all of the Hebrew Scriptures, or anything evenly remotely close to the sentence, "He shall be called a Nazarene." In the entire Hebrew Scriptures, there is no use of the word "Nazarene," nor is there any mention of any city or place named "Nazareth."

Matthew 2:23 *And he came and dwelt in a city called Nazareth: that it might be fulfilled which was spoken by the prophets, He shall be called a Nazarene.*

Christians will respond by saying that the New Testament was referring to Jesus as a branch, which in Hebrew is "netzer," or they will say it refers to Jesus being like a Nazir, one who took a Nazarite vow. This is not the issue at hand. The question is, Matthew makes it look as though Jesus fulfilled an explicit verse found in a Biblical Prophet. Where is that verse? It does not exist.

Inventions of Stories to Fit Verses

The fact that stories about Jesus were invented to make it look as though Jesus fulfilled a prophecy concerning the Messiah found in the Hebrew Scriptures can best be shown by comparing stories in one Gospel with the same rendition of the story in another Gospel.

Our first example will be to look at the two versions of the birth stories of Jesus, found in Matthew and in Luke. Our second example will be to look at the stories of Jesus' first entrance into Jerusalem in Matthew and in Mark.

There are two birth stories in the New Testament, one in Matthew and one in Luke, but they hardly tell the same story. No one can write a single narrative that takes into account each and every element of these two birth stories of Jesus, because the stories disagree too often with each other.

In Matthew's version, Jesus is born during a time of fear, with Herod searching after Jesus to kill him, leading to Joseph and Mary fleeing into Egypt with Jesus. However, the mood painted by Luke is that it was a time of peace with shepherds herding their flocks in the Judean hills with nothing written regarding Herod's search. In Matthew, Jesus is born at home, since Joseph and Mary were from Bethlehem, while in Luke, Joseph and Mary had to take a trip to Bethlehem from Nazareth, and Mary had to give birth to Jesus in a manger because there was no room at the Inn. Matthew speaks of a star while Luke says nothing of it (and that star was seen in the

East, while the wise men were East of Bethlehem!). Matthew speaks of Wise Men searching for Jesus, while Luke speaks of shepherds coming to visit Jesus. Did Luke not need them to be Wise Men, wise in the ways of astrology, since he did not say anything about a star?

Had these stories not been simply made up (most likely to show that Jesus, too, had a miracle birth like the pagan gods of that day) they would have agreed on many more details, especially if these texts really were "the Gospel truth."

Therefore remember that when a Christian missionary, or missionary literature, tries to tell you that a story about Jesus is reflected in a story from the Hebrew Scriptures, see if there is another version of this story in another part of the Christian's New Testament. If the two versions are not exactly the same, then the stories could have been made up to make it look like Jesus fulfilled those verses.

Furthermore, remember that since the time of Jesus there have been 14 people who claimed to have been the Jewish Messiah. Not one of them felt obligated to claim to have been born of a virgin (or, for that matter, to have been born in Bethlehem!) because Jews have never believed that the Messiah will be born of a virgin. Being born of a virgin would preclude that child from ever being the messiah, as we discussed in Chapter 9.

As a second example of stories that were made up regarding Jesus to show that he fulfilled Biblical verses, let us look at two versions of the story of the first entrance of Jesus into Jerusalem. Matthew describes Jesus riding upon two animals while Mark describes Jesus riding upon one animal:

> Matthew 21:1-7 *And when they drew nigh unto Jerusalem, and were come to Bethphage, unto the mount of Olives, then sent Jesus two disciples, 2 Saying unto them, Go into the village over against you, and straightway ye shall find **an ass tied, and a colt with her**: loose **them**, and bring **them** unto me. 3 And if any man say ought unto you, ye shall say, The Lord hath need of **them**; and*

*straightway he will send **them**. 4 All this was done, that it might be fulfilled which was spoken by the prophet, saying, 5 Tell ye the daughter of Sion, Behold, thy King cometh unto thee, meek, and sitting upon an ass, and a colt the foal of an ass. 6 And the disciples went, and did as Jesus commanded them, 7 And brought **the ass, and the colt**, and put on **them** their clothes, and they set him thereon.*

*Mark 11:1-7 And when they came nigh to Jerusalem, unto Bethphage and Bethany, at the mount of Olives, he sendeth forth two of his disciples, 2 And saith unto them, Go your way into the village over against you: and as soon as ye be entered into it, ye shall find **a colt tied**, whereon never man sat; loose **him**, and bring **him**. 3 And if any man say unto you, Why do ye this? say ye that the Lord hath need of **him**; and straightway he will send **him** hither. 4 And they went their way, and found **the colt tied** by the door without in a place where two ways met; and they loose **him**. 5 And certain of them that stood there said unto them, What do ye, loosing **the colt**? 6 And they said unto them even as Jesus had commanded: and they let them go. 7 And they brought **the colt** to Jesus, and cast their garments on **him**; and he sat upon **him**.*

Why is it that the two stories, supposedly describing eyewitness reports of the same event, are different? Of course one might respond by saying that eyewitnesses will describe the same event differently. But these stories are supposed to be "Gospel Truth" and inspired by God. Matthew again makes it seem as though Jesus were fulfilling a prophecy concerning the Messiah by riding upon two animals. If this is indeed a prophecy, then according to Mark, Jesus did not fulfill the prophecy because according to Mark, Jesus entered Jerusalem while riding on only one animal.

Why then is there a difference between the two stories? To understand this you must examine the source of the prophecy concerning the Messiah, Zechariah 9:9-10:

9 Rejoice greatly, O Daughter of Zion! Shout a loud, O daughter of Jerusalem! Lo, your king comes to you; triuphant and victorious is he, humble and riding on an ass, on a colt, the foal of an ass. 10 I will cut off the chariot from Ephraim, and the war horse from Jerusalem; and the battle bow shall be cut off, and he shall command peace to the nations; his dominion shall be from sea to sea, and from the River to the ends of the earth.

When Zechariah wrote in verse 9 above, "riding on an ass, on a colt, the foal of an ass," was he talking about one ass or was he talking about two asses? Matthew understood Zechariah to be talking about two animals, so he wrote his story about Jesus riding on two. Mark understood Zechariah to be talking about one animal, so he wrote his story about Jesus riding on one.

Zechariah was talking about only one animal. He was using the ancient form of Hebrew poetry which involves a rhyming by repetition of ideas, by repeating the same idea but by using different words, and not a rhyming of sounds. This Biblical poetry is called Parallelism. Look at almost any Psalm and you will see this clearly. For example, read Psalm 19:7:

The law of the Eternal is perfect, converting the soul: the testimony of the Eternal is sure, making wise the simple.

In the verse above, "the law of the Eternal" is parallel to "the testimony of the Eternal," and "perfect" is parallel to "sure," and "converting the soul" is parallel to "making wise the simple."

The Zechariah quotation also tells us that the Messiah "commands peace to the nations," and that the Messiah shall rule "from sea to sea." Jesus said in Matthew 10:34, that his purpose in coming was to bring a sword and not to bring peace, nor did Jesus ever rule from sea to sea, except in the minds of believing Christians.

When a Christian missionary, or missionary literature, tries to tell you that a story about Jesus is reflected in a story or verse from the Hebrew Scriptures, see if there is another version of this story in another part of the Christian's New Testament. If the two versions are not exactly the same, then each of the stories could have been made up independently of each other, to make it look like Jesus fulfilled something in the Hebrew Scriptures.

D. Typologies

What is a Typology? A typology is where a story or narrative or even a character in the Hebrew Scriptures is seen as a type or model, like a prophecy or pre-figuring or foreshadowing, of the story or narrative or character of Jesus.

A perfect example of this can be seen in Matthew, where Jesus likens himself and what is to happen to him, to the story of Jonah:

> Matthew 12:38-40 *Then certain of the scribes and of the Pharisees answered, saying, Master, we would see a sign from thee. 39 But he answered and said unto them, An evil and adulterous generation seeketh after a sign; and there shall no sign be given to it, but the sign of the prophet Jonah: 40 For as Jonah was three days and three nights in the whale's belly; so shall the Son of man be three days and three nights in the heart of the earth.*

Above, the narrative of Jesus uses the story of Jonah to make it appear that the theology of Christianity, the death and resurrection of Jesus, is pre-figured or foreshadowed in that story of Jonah.

There are problems with using typologies. A typology may make it appear that a Biblical story is a kind of a prophecy of Jesus, but upon closer examination, the two stories are nothing like each other.

The following anecdote exemplifies this:

One day, Jesus was in heaven and decided to look up his earthly father. So, he went to the area of Heaven reserved for carpenters. He came upon a carpenter and began a conversation with him. In the course of their conversation, Jesus asked him, "Did you have any children?" At this question, the carpenter brightened up, and said, "Oh, yes, I had a son and he was very special!" At this, Jesus brightened up and asked, "Really!? What made him so special?" The carpenter responded, "Well, he was thought to have been human, but he did not start out that way. He had holes in his hands and his feet, and he died and he came back to life!" Jesus ran to hug the man and exclaimed, "Father!" and the carpenter ran to Jesus and shouted, "Pinocchio!"

At first glance, it is true that the description of Pinocchio did, indeed, sound like the description of Jesus. Pinocchio began his life made from wood, and became human, while Jesus, according to Christianity, began as God, and became human. Pinocchio had holes in his hands and feet because he was a puppet, while Jesus had holes in his hands and feet from the crucifixion. Pinocchio died, but the Blue Fairy brought him back to life as a real boy, while Jesus, according to Christian beliefs died and came back to life when he was resurrected. However, upon closer examination of the lives of Pinocchio and Jesus, they were nothing alike.

Similarly, if one were to closely examine the stories used as typologies taken from the Hebrew Scriptures and compare them with the life of Jesus, one would see that they, too, do not match.

For example in the use of the story of Jonah, above, Jesus explicitly states that, like Jonah who was in the belly of the whale for three days and three nights, Jesus would be buried in the earth for three days and for three nights. However, if one simply remembers the story of Jesus as portrayed in the Christians' New Testament and the way in which it is celebrated all over the world, Jesus was crucified and buried on a Friday (called Good Friday), and was resurrected on a Sunday (called Easter Sunday):

Friday - the first day
Friday Night - the first night
Saturday - the second day
Saturday night - the second night
Sunday morning - Jesus was resurrected

But if on Sunday, at some point during the day, he was supposedly resurrected, where is the third night? Jesus, according to the story in Matthew, did not even fulfill his own typology or prophecy of being in the earth for three days and three nights as Jonah was in the whale for that length of time.

In John, this problem is made worse, because according to John, Jesus spent no part of the day of Sunday in the earth, because the tomb was already empty before sunrise:

> John 20:1-2 *The first day of the week cometh Mary Magdalene early, when it was yet dark, unto the sepulchre, and seeth the stone taken away from the sepulchre. 2 Then she runneth, and cometh to Simon Peter, and to the other disciple, whom Jesus loved, and saith unto them, They have taken away the Lord out of the sepulchre, and we know not where they have laid him.*

This would mean that according to John, Jesus was only buried for two days and two nights.

Typologies at first glance may seem to reflect the story of Jesus, but upon further examination, a closer look at the typology and the story of Jesus, they do not match, and the Biblical story is not useful as a pre-figuring of the life of Jesus.

CHAPTER 14

THE TEN MOST COMMONLY USED PROOFTEXTS

In the context of this discussion, a prooftext is a verse, or verses, taken from the Hebrew Scriptures that Christians believe were meant to be a prophecy of the messiah, and which were fulfilled by Jesus. These prooftexts are used to prove that what Christians believe is reflected in the Hebrew Scriptures.

Regarding the verses in the Hebrew Scriptures, there are 4 kinds of verses:

1. Verses that both Jews and Christians agree have nothing to do with the messiah. Although it is true that any verse can be interpreted to have something to do with the messiah, there are verses which no one believes do so.

2. Verses that both Jews and Christians believe are related to the messiah, or to the period or events that involve the messiah.

3. Verses that Christians say are related to the messiah, while Jews do not.

4. Verses that Jews say are related to the messiah, while Christians do not.

It is interesting to note that the verses that both Jews and Christians agree are messianic, having something to do with the messiah or his coming, have yet to be fulfilled. Therefore Christians invented the idea of a Second Coming, that Jesus will do all those things that remain to be done when he returns.

The verses that Christians use as Prooftexts, usually fall under the third category above.

Although one could give a Christian interpretation to any and every verse of the Bible, for our purposes we are only going to look at ten of the most commonly used verses from the Hebrew Scriptures that Christians use to proselytize Jews to Christianity, and the Jewish response. Please review the bibliography for references to other books that give a more complete response.

When one compares the interpretation given by Christians to these verses, to the simple plain meaning of the verses in question, or to other verses in the Hebrew Scriptures, or to verses in the Christian's New Testament itself, one can see that the Christian interpretation is not valid or that Jesus did not fulfill it. Please refer to the Introduction to this book to fully understand this point. We are going to provide another interpretation, one that, unlike the Christian interpretation, conforms to the beliefs and values set forth by other verses in the Bible. This demonstrates that there is an alternative interpretation that is more valid than the Christian interpretation because it conforms to the beliefs and values set forth by other verses in the Bible.

1. Genesis 1:1

Genesis 1:1 *In the beginning God created the heaven and the earth.*

When one reads the very first verse of the Bible, one may not see how this verse could possibly be used by Christianity to prove a Christian claim. However, Christians see in this verse an indication of the Trinity, the belief that God is made up of three "persons," "the Father, the Son, and the Holy Spirit." To understand how

Christians see this in this verse, one must read it in the original Hebrew. Transliterated for the purposes of this book, it reads,

B'raysheet Bara Eloheem Et Hashamayim V'et Ha-aretz.

Christians see that the word in the verse used for "God," is the word "Eloheem." They point out that the ending of "eem" indicates a plural in the Hebrew language, and they are right, usually the "eem" at the end of the word indicates a plural. For example, "sefer" is "book," while "sefareem," is "books."

However, not all words with "eem" on the end are plural. For example, the word "ma-yeem" is "water," and not "waters." The same is true for the word, "paneem," which means "face" and not "faces."

In the above examples, the verbs and adjectives that would be used for the subject of "pa-neem" and for "ma-yeem" would have to match, and would both have to be plural. However, the verb in Genesis 1:1 is "bara," and is not in the plural, which would be "bar-u." This means that the Hebrew does not recognize the word for God, "Eloheem," to be in the plural.

The most important response to this Christian claim is to understand that there is no reason to assume a plural reference to God must mean three. A plural is simply more than one, and can indicate 2, 3, 5, or even 235,000. There is nothing to indicate that any plural reference to God must specifically mean three. If one was required to see plurals in relationship to God, to be references to a Trinity, would that mean that someone with a "paneem," a "face" in Hebrew, would actually mean that person was three-faced?

As we said in the introduction to this section, the way in which someone interprets a Biblical verse will be influenced by the reader's experiences and beliefs. A Christian assumes that the plural references to God always mean three, because a Christian begins with the assumption that God is a Trinity. However, what if a Hindu, with their belief in multiple gods read the same verse? The Hindu certainly could claim that the verse referred to the multiplicity of Hindu gods, while the Christian would claim that the verse referred to their Trinity, and the Jew will maintain that it refers to an absolute one God. Of course, the Jewish claim will be based on the verb being in the singular, and the existence of other words that, like Eloheem, appear to be plural but are not. Furthermore, the Jewish claim will be based on the Jewish idea of absolute Monotheism, that God is One and indivisible. However, the Christian and the Hindu are free to reject the Jewish claim, which is what makes them Christians or Hindus.

It also must be noted that the word "Eloheem" is also used in the Bible to refer to pagan idols. In the Ten Commandments we read,

> Exodus 20:3 *Thou shalt have no other gods <eloheem> before me.*

To be accurate, the word, "Eloheem" comes from the root which means "power." The Bible uses the word "Eloheem" to mean God, because God is the Ultimate Power, however when it does so, it uses a verb that is singular, not recognizing the subject, "Eloheem" as plural.

2. Genesis 1:26

One sees the same problem resulting in a plural reference to God, in another verse commonly used by Christians to prove that their concept of the Trinity is to be found in the Hebrew Scriptures.

> Genesis 1:26 *And God said, Let us make man in our image, after our likeness: and let them have dominion over the fish of the sea, and over the fowl of the air, and over the cattle, and over all the earth, and over every creeping thing that creepeth upon the earth.*

Because the above also refers to God in the plural, "Let *us* make man in *our* image . . . ," Christians will claim that this plural reference to God indicates their Trinity. However the same objection mentioned above regarding Genesis 1:1 can also be applied here. Just because the term 'us,' referring to God is in the plural, it does not necessarily have to mean a Trinity. Plurals are more than one, and this plural can also be interpreted to mean 2 or 3 or 3 million. It can also be interpreted by Hindus to indicate the multiplicity of their gods, as well.

To understand the Jewish interpretation of this verse, it should be known that in the preceding verses, God had called upon the Earth to aid in the creation of plant life as well as the creation of the other living creatures:

> Genesis 1:11-12 *11 And God said, Let the earth bring forth grass, the herb yielding seed, and the fruit tree yielding fruit after his kind, whose seed is in itself, upon the earth: and it was so. 12 And the earth brought forth grass, and herb yielding seed after his kind, and the tree yielding fruit, whose seed was in itself, after his kind: and God saw that it was good.*

> Genesis 1:24-25 *24 And God said, Let the earth bring forth the living creature after his kind, cattle, and creeping thing, and beast of the earth after his kind: and it was so. 25 And God made the beast of the earth after his kind, and cattle after their kind, and every thing that creepeth upon the earth after his kind: and God saw that it was good.*

Judaism believes that human beings are made up of both flesh and blood, the material, as well as the soul, the spiritual. The Earth provides the material while God provides the soul, the spiritual. Furthermore, when a person dies, Judaism believes that the flesh and blood of the deceased goes back to the earth, while the soul returns to God. This is seen in Ecclesiastes 12:7, where it explicitly states this:

> *Then shall the dust return to the earth as it was: and the spirit shall return unto God who gave it.*

From the Jewish perspective, God was speaking to the Earth when He said "Let us make man . . ." which is evidenced in the

Biblical account just a few verses before when he also used the Earth in the creation of plants and animals. There are other, equally valid, Jewish interpretations of this verse from Genesis, and each one will maintain the Bible's absolute monotheism. The interpretation discussed above is just the simplest and most easily explained, and it is proved by the verses preceding the verse in question. For other equally valid Jewish interpretations of these verses, see the Bibliography.

3. Genesis 3:22

And again, in the following verses, Christians will see the use of a plural in relation to God, and assume that it means the Trinity.

> Gen 3:22-24 *22 And the Eternal God said, Behold, the man is become as one of us, to know good and evil: and now, lest he put forth his hand, and take also of the tree of life, and eat, and live for ever: 23 Therefore the Eternal God sent him forth from the garden of Eden, to till the ground from whence he was taken. 24 So he drove out the man; and he placed at the east of the garden of Eden Cherubims, and a flaming sword which turned every way, to keep the way of the tree of life.*

God could have been using what is called the "pluralis majestatis," the "majestic plural," or the "royal 'we.'" Many are familiar with the statement made by Queen Victoria in the early 1900's, "We are not amused," referring to herself. Again, even if this were a plural reference to God, it doesn't have to mean three, it could mean three thousand. If Hindus were to interpret these verses saying that it refers to the multiplicity of Hindu gods, how could a Christian claim that the Hindu interpretation was any less valid than their own?

There is a more obvious meaning to be found in the entire passage and in the simple meaning of the verses. God is speaking to someone (or to some) who, like God, know the difference between Good and

Evil, and who, like God, are immortal. Just a few verses before Genesis 3:22, God had already created the angels, the hosts of heaven.

> Genesis 2:1 *Thus the heavens and the earth were finished, and all the host of them.*

From the Jewish perspective, in Genesis 3:22, God was speaking to the Heavenly Hosts, the angels. The angels, like God, are immortal, and, like God, they know the difference between Good and Evil. This is what the verses here are saying. Adam and Eve ate the fruit of The Tree of the Knowledge of the Difference Between Good and Evil, and therefore know the difference between Good and Evil. However, unlike God and the angels, Adam and Eve remain mortal. If they were to then eat from the Tree of Life, they would become immortal, and so God separates them from the Tree of Life by removing them from of the Garden of Eden, and then keeps them away from the Tree of Life by placing Cherubim with flaming swords to guard the way to the Tree of Life. This is exactly and explicitly what the verses state:

> 22 . . . *lest he put forth his hand, and take also of the tree of life, and eat, and live for ever: 23 Therefore the Eternal God sent him forth from the garden of Eden, to till the ground from whence he was taken. 24 So he drove out the man; and he placed at the east of the garden of Eden Cherubims, and a flaming sword which turned every way, to keep the way of the tree of life.*

Again and again, just because there is some use of a plural word in relation to God, it does not mean a Trinity. By looking at the verse in context, or knowing the original language, we can see that the Jewish understanding of the verse will remain in keeping with the absolute monotheism that is found in the rest of the Biblical text.

4. Genesis 49:10

Christians understand the following verse to mean that when the Messiah comes, whom they believe to have been Jesus, the kingship will no longer belong to the tribe of Judah, and that the rule of the Jews over their own Promised Land will end.

> Genesis 49:10 *The sceptre shall not depart from Judah, nor a lawgiver from between his feet, until Shiloh come; and unto him shall the gathering of the people be.*

The sceptre is the symbol of royal power. When the text reads that "the sceptre shall not depart from Judah . . . until Shiloh come," Christians interpret this to mean that when Shiloh comes, whom they believe to mean their messiah Jesus, then the rule of the Tribe of Judah will end. Since the Jews were exiled from the Promised Land almost 40 years after Jesus came, Christians will say that this prophecy was fulfilled at the coming of Jesus.

However, there are a few things wrong with this interpretation.

If I were to say to you "there will be money in your bank account until you get paid," would that mean that after you get paid there will no longer be any money in your bank account? Wouldn't that mean, instead, that even after you got paid there would still be money in your bank account? The Messiah is supposed to reign over Israel and he is supposed to be from the Tribe of Judah, which means that until the Messiah comes, and even after the Messiah comes, the sceptre will still belong to a member of the Tribe of Judah, namely to the Messiah.

Secondly, even if Jesus had been the Messiah, according to Christianity, Jesus was supposedly from the tribe of Judah, and so the sceptre would still belong to Judah during Jesus' "reign," although Jesus never reigned over anything except in the minds of Christians. For the Jews, the Messiah has yet to come, and so until he comes, the sceptre belongs to him, and when the real messiah comes, the sceptre will still be his.

The biggest problem with the Christian interpretation is that in the year 586 B.C.E., the Babylonians overcame Jerusalem, carried off King Zedekiah into exile, and destroyed the Temple. Zedekiah was the last descendant of King David to sit upon the throne over the Promised Land. Since the Babylonians, there have been a long succession of foreign domination over the Land of Israel: the Persians, then the Greeks, then the Romans (who had been ruling the land of Israel for 64 years before Jesus was born), then the Turks, and then the English. During these periods of foreign rule over the Promised Land, there might have occasionally been a Jew to govern the land for the foreign powers; however there was no Jewish King who alone had sovereignty over the land. Historically, therefore, even if one agreed with the Christian interpretation of this verse, then "the sceptre" had "departed from Judah" almost 600 years before Jesus was born when Zedekiah's reign ended.

5. Leviticus 17:11

This verse was discussed at length in Chapter 7. However, for the purposes of the discussion of comparing interpretations, we will look at it here, as well.

Christians believe that in order for one to be forgiven of one's sins, there has to be a blood sacrifice. This is how they interpret Leviticus 17:11, which reads:

> For the life of the flesh is in the blood: and I have given
> it to you upon the altar to make an atonement for your souls:
> for it is the blood that maketh an atonement for the soul.

Taken out of context, one could understand this quotation in the same way as the Christians. However, when you read the entire passage from Leviticus, you will see that this verse is part of a whole passage that is simply trying to say that one is not to drink the blood of any sacrifice, as the pagans of that period used to do.

> Leviticus 17:10-12 *10 And whatsoever man there be*
> *of the house of Israel, or of the strangers that sojourn among*

you, that eateth any manner of blood; I will even set my face against that soul that eateth blood, and will cut him off from among his people. 11 For the life of the flesh is in the blood: and I have given it to you upon the altar to make an atonement for your souls: for it is the blood that maketh an atonement for the soul. 12 Therefore I said unto the children of Israel, No soul of you shall eat blood, neither shall any stranger that sojourneth among you eat blood.

Often, when Christians use verses to try to convert Jews, they will only show you a single verse. Always look at the entire context in which that verse is found, because the context may show that the Christian interpretation is simply a misinterpretation.

At the time in which Jesus lived, 80% of all the Jews in the world lived outside the land of Israel, away from Jerusalem, away from the Temple, without the ability to perform any animal sacrifices. They did not live in the fear that their sins were not forgiven by God. The reason for this is quite simply that the Jews never felt that animal sacrifices were the only means to forgiveness.

Christians claim that one must have a blood sacrifice for the forgiveness of sin. However, if one can see even one place in the Hebrew Scriptures where God forgives sin without a blood sacrifice, then one does not have to have a blood sacrifice to be forgiven. And there are many, many quotations throughout the entire Bible that prove this point. Because this was discussed at length in Chapter 7, we will only look at a few.

It is in the Book of Leviticus where the whole of the sacrificial system is discussed. And in Leviticus, right in the midst of the description of the sacrifices, we have a quotation that proves that blood sacrifices are not necessary for the forgiveness of sin.

Leviticus 5:11-13 *But if he be not able to bring two turtledoves, or two young pigeons, then he that sinned shall bring for his offering the tenth part of an ephah of fine flour for a sin offering; he shall put no oil upon it, neither shall he put any frankincense thereon: for it is a sin offering. 12*

Then shall he bring it to the priest, and the priest shall take his handful of it, even a memorial thereof, and burn it on the altar, according to the offerings made by fire unto the Eternal: it is a sin offering. 13 And the priest shall make an atonement for him as touching his sin that he hath sinned in one of these, and it shall be forgiven him: and the remnant shall be the priest's, as a meat offering.

Thus we see that if someone could not afford any of the animals, that the offering of flour would attain for him the same forgiveness that the animal sacrifices would bring. Flour has no blood, flour has no life to be sacrificed, and yet with the sacrifice of the flour the sinner would still be forgiven. If, in fact, a blood sacrifice was absolutely necessary for the forgiveness of sin, then the use of flour would not have been possible, even if it was only for the poor.

We have another example of the forgiveness of sin without the need of any blood sacrifice. In the Book of Jonah we read how Jonah was told by God to go to the Ninevites to get them to repent of their sins. Jonah did not like the people of Ninevah. He knew that they would repent if he warned them, but he preferred their destruction. Jonah tried to run away from God, but instead was brought back to the land in the belly of the great fish. Jonah then obeyed God and came to Ninevah. There, he warned them of God's intent to destroy them if they did not seek atonement for their sins. The people, from the King on down, prayed to God for forgiveness, fasted by neither eating nor drinking, and they stopped their evil ways. And then what happened?

Jonah 3:10 *And God saw their works, that they turned from their evil way; and God repented of the evil, that he had said that he would do unto them; and he did it not.*

The people of Ninevah did not perform any sacrifices. They did much the same as the Jews do all over the world on the Day of Atonement, spending the day in prayer and fasting. The People of Ninevah were forgiven for their sins without the need of any blood sacrifice, just as we, now, are forgiven for our sins without the need of any blood sacrifice.

Most people are aware of the function of the scapegoat described in Leviticus 16:20-22. The sins of the people were symbolically placed on the head of the goat who was then banished to the wilderness. Even though the ritual described in the Bible does not call for the goat to be killed, even though there was no blood sacrifice, the sins of the people were forgiven.

Similarly, most people know that the blood sacrifices were to take place only in the Temple which was built by Solomon. In I Kings 8, Solomon dedicates the Temple to the One True God, the only Temple on Earth dedicated to the One, True God. At that dedication, Solomon states that there would come a time when the Jews, as a result of their sins, would be exiled from the Promised Land. He prayed that when they were in the land of their enemies, that all they would have to do to be forgiven of their sins was to pray, and to pray towards the Temple (which is why Synagogues and Temples face East, when they are in the West), to repent of their sins, and to stop sinning, just as we learned above from Jonah.

1 Kings 8:46-50 *46 If they sin against thee, (for there is no man that sinneth not,) and thou be angry with them, and deliver them to the enemy, so that they carry them away captives unto the land of the enemy, far or near; 47 Yet if they shall bethink themselves in the land whither they were carried captives, and repent, and make supplication unto thee in the land of them that carried them captives, saying, We have sinned, and have done perversely, we have committed wickedness; 48 And so return unto thee with all their heart, and with all their soul, in the land of their enemies, which led them away captive, and pray unto thee toward their land, which thou gavest unto their fathers, the city which thou hast chosen, and the house which I have built for thy name: 49 Then hear thou their prayer and their supplication in heaven thy dwelling place, and maintain their cause, 50 And forgive thy people that have*

*sinned against thee, and all their transgressions wherein they
have transgressed against thee, and give them compassion
before them who carried them captive, that they may have
compassion on them:*

The interesting thing about the above verses is that Solomon, who offered this prayer at the dedication of the very place where the blood sacrifices were to be offered, had to have known that a blood sacrifice was not necessary for atonement. Had he felt that a blood sacrifice was necessary, he would not have bothered praying this prayer. Indeed, God does forgive our sins and grant us atonement when we repent, when we confess our sins, when we pray for forgiveness, and when we do not do the sin again when given the chance.

There are many other places in the Bible where the sins were forgiven without the need of a blood sacrifice of an animal. One can see that, since the Bible never claimed that one required a blood sacrifice for the forgiveness of sin, the Christian interpretation of Leviticus 17:11 is unbiblical.

6. Isaiah 9:6-7

Isaiah 9:6-7 *For unto us a child is born, unto us a son
is given: and the government shall be upon his shoulder:
and his name shall be called Wonderful, Counselor, The
Mighty God, The Everlasting Father, The Prince of Peace.
7 Of the increase of his government and peace there shall be
no end, upon the throne of David, and upon his kingdom,
to order it, and to establish it with judgment and with
justice from henceforth even forever. The zeal of the Eternal
of hosts will perform this.*

Christians see the above verses from Isaiah 9 to be speaking of Jesus, who came into the world as a child. However, after having read the above quotation, a few questions should come to mind.

When did Jesus ever run any government?

When was Jesus ever called a "Wonderful Counselor," or a "Mighty God," or an "Everlasting Father," or a "Prince of Peace?" Jesus was never called by any of these names anywhere in the Christian's New Testament and not at all in his own lifetime.

Christians always seem to misunderstand this quotation. This is because they do not understand Hebrew, nor do they understand names, nor do they understand Hebrew names.

In any language, every name has a meaning. The name "Anthony" means "priceless," and the name "Alexander" means "protector." If we were to give a child the first and middle names of Anthony Alexander, would that mean that we are saying that this child is "a priceless protector?" Would we call out to him, "Hey, Priceless Protector, how are you?" Of course not. We would use his names, and not the meaning of his names.

Hebrew names sometimes say something about God. The name Michael means "who is like God." The name Elihu means "my God is He," or "He is my God." The name Immanuel means "God is with us," just to give a few examples. If someone has the name, Elihu, (again, meaning "He is my God") would that mean that the human being known as Elihu is God? These names say something about God, even though they are the names of ordinary human beings. A better translation to the verse in question might be "and his name will be called, 'A wonderful counselor is the mighty God, an everlasting father is the ruler of peace.'" This means that there are really only two Hebrew names in the verse, which are given to a human being and not to a divine being, even though the names make a statement about God. Those names, like Anthony Alexander in our example above, would be "Pele Yoetz El Gibor Avi Ad Sar Shalom." The way it is written in the original Hebrew, the names would be hyphenated as "Pele-Yoetz-El-Gibor" and "Avi-Ad-Sar-Shalom." Lengthy names like these were not uncommon in the Bible, and in Isaiah specifically. For example, in Isaiah 8:3, we find the name, "Maher-shalal-chash-baz," which means "the spoil speeds, the pray hastens."

The Christian interpretation of Isaiah 9:6 is that Jesus was a Wonderful Counselor, a Mighty God, an Everlasting Father, and a

Prince of Peace. How well would these descriptive names apply to Jesus? Is this similar to the story of Pinocchio, as we discussed in the Introduction to Section II, under Typologies? Is the description of the person described in Isaiah 9:6-7, which at first sounds like the story of Jesus, on closer examination found to be inaccurate?

"Wonderful Counselor"

In the Christian's New Testament we find two stories about Jesus that certainly do not describe him as a Wonderful Counselor:

> Matthew 8:21-22 *And another of his disciples said unto him, Lord, suffer me first to go and bury my father. 22 But Jesus said unto him, Follow me; and let the dead bury their dead.*

A "Wonderful Counselor" would not tell a man who had recently lost his beloved father not to see to his father's funeral.

> John 18:22-23 *And when he had thus spoken, one of the officers which stood by struck Jesus with the palm of his hand, saying, Answerest thou the high priest so? 23 Jesus answered him, If I have spoken evil, bear witness of the evil: but if well, why smitest thou me?*

Everyone is familiar with the quotation from Jesus, "*Do not resist one who is evil, but if anyone strikes you on the right cheek, turn to him the other also,*" found in Matthew 5:39. In the quotation above from John 18, Jesus does not turn his other cheek to the one who struck him, but rebukes him instead. One who says one thing but does another is called a hypocrite, and how can a hypocrite be a "Wonderful Counselor?"

"Mighty God."

Matthew 27:46 *And about the ninth hour Jesus cried with a loud voice, saying, Eli, Eli, lama sabachthani? that is to say, My God, my God, why hast thou forsaken me?*

If Jesus were the "Mighty God," why would he have to call upon another as God in order to save him? How can God forsake himself? This also denies the very idea of a trinity, and shows how Jesus does not fit the description of Isaiah 9:6.

Matthew 19:16-17 *And, behold, one came and said unto him, Good Master, what good thing shall I do, that I may have eternal life? 17 And he said unto him, Why callest thou me good? there is none good but one, that is, God: but if thou wilt enter into life, keep the commandments.*

In the above verses, Jesus distinguishes between himself and God. How could he have been the "Mighty God," if he himself made a distinction between himself and God? If Jesus knew that only God is good, and that he should not be called good, then Jesus knew that Jesus was not God.

"Everlasting Father"

Out of the Trinity, Jesus is the son, and not the Father. He cannot be both at the same time. As a matter of fact, Jesus himself showed that he was not the Father, and claimed not to have the same will, or the same knowledge as the Father.

Matthew 26:39 *And he went a little further, and fell on his face, and prayed, saying, O my Father, if it be possible, let this cup pass from me: nevertheless not as I will, but as thou wilt.*

Jesus calls the One to whom he prayed his Father, so Jesus cannot be "the Everlasting Father," if he called another his Father. Jesus could not be the Father if the will of Jesus is not the same as the will of the Father. Jesus and the Father are separate and unequal, and this denies the very idea of the trinity.

> Mark 13:32 *But of that day and that hour knoweth no man, no, not the angels which are in heaven, neither the Son, but the Father.*

In the above verse, Jesus claims there is something that he does not know, but that only the Father knows. Jesus, "the son," cannot also be the Father if their knowledge is not the same.

> John 20:17 *Jesus saith unto her, Touch me not; for I am not yet ascended to my Father: but go to my brethren, and say unto them, I ascend unto my Father, and your Father; and to my God, and your God.*

How can the Father ascend to Himself? In the above verse, Jesus not only distinguishes between himself and his Father, but he also makes it sound as though the relationship that he has with the Father, is exactly the same relationship that all people have with God, who is, in fact, the Father of all.

"Prince of Peace"

The last descriptive name from Isaiah 9:6 that Christians say refers to Jesus is "Prince of Peace." However, this is a mistranslation. The words in the original Hebrew are, "sar shalom." The word "sar" does not mean "prince," it means "ruler." Now, one might say that a "prince" is a "ruler." However, the reason why the Christians choose the word "prince" instead of the word "ruler" in Christian translations is that the word "prince" makes one think that the original verse is speaking of a "son of the king." In the Christian mind this alludes to Jesus whom they believe to have been the son of God, the King. However, the word is "ruler," and not "prince." "Prince" in Hebrew is "naseech" and not "sar." The Christian translators intentionally chose the English word "prince" to lead the reader into thinking about Jesus.

In the Christian's New Testament, we also find a quotation which certainly does not show Jesus to have been a "ruler" or even a "prince" of peace.

> Matthew 10:34-36 *Think not that I am come to send peace on earth: I came not to send peace, but a sword. 35 For I am come to set a man at variance against his father, and the daughter against her mother, and the daughter in law against her mother in law. 36 And a man's foes shall be they of his own household.*

No one who said such a thing can be considered a prince or ruler of peace. No one who said such a thing could have been the Messiah. We know that the true Messiah will bring an everlasting peace and, along with Elijah the Prophet, will bring families closer to each other and not further apart (see Isaiah 2:4, Micah 4:1-4, and Malachi 4:5).

I have already stated that Christians rarely include verse 7 when they quote Isaiah 9. The reason is that in verse 7 it states, "Of the increase of his government and of peace there will be no end." Perhaps they do not quote verse 7 because Jesus never brought peace to the world, nor did he ever intend to, as the above quotation from Matthew 10:34-36 shows.

Jesus was also a violent man, and not a "Prince of Peace," or even a "Ruler of Peace." There are other verses in the Christian's New Testament that indicates this. Here are two more:

> Luke 19:27 *But those mine enemies, which would not that I should reign over them, bring hither, and slay them before me.*

The verse above comes at the end of a parable that Jesus told of a man that leaves his land to go to be anointed as the King. When he comes back to his land, he says the above. Every single Christian commentator claims that Jesus was referring to himself as the man who left his land to be anointed King, and so in his own parable, Jesus is saying the above, asking that those who do not wish to have him reign over them be murdered in front of him.

In the verse, below, Jesus tells his followers to go and buy a sword.

> Luke 22:35 *And he said unto them, When I sent you without purse, and scrip, and shoes, lacked ye any thing? And they said, Nothing. 36 Then said he unto them, But now, he that hath a purse, let him take it, and likewise his scrip: and he that hath no sword, let him sell his garment, and buy one.*

We have shown from quotations from the Christian's New Testament that Jesus was not a "Wonderful Counselor," Jesus was not a "Mighty God," Jesus was not an "Everlasting Father," nor was Jesus a "Prince of Peace" or even a "Ruler of Peace," in spite of how Christians wish to interpret the original verses from Isaiah 9:6-7.

So, according to the Jewish interpretation, who is Isaiah 9:6-7 speaking about?

According to Judaism, the answer is in the names chosen. The name "Hezekiah," which in Hebrew is "Chizkiyah," comes from the words "chazak" and "Ya." "Chazak" means "strong" or "mighty" and "Ya" is the shortened name for God used as a suffix. Many might recognize the word, "Ya," in the word, "halleluyah," which means, "praise God." Judaism believes that Isaiah 9:6-7 refers to Hezekiah, who reigned for almost 30 years. The name Hezekiah, Chizkiyah, is the same name in meaning as one finds in the verses from Isaiah 9:6-7, a "Mighty God."

7. Jeremiah 31:31-34

Jeremiah 31:31-34 speaks of a "new covenant," and the term "covenant" means "testament." So, in these verses, Christians see a prophecy of their New Testament, as Paul referring to Jeremiah 31:31 writes in Hebrews 8:13:

> *In that he saith, A new covenant, he hath made the first old. Now that which decayeth and waxeth old is ready to vanish away.*

Have you ever seen an advertisement on television where a manufacturer has come out with the new and improved version of a product they are already known for, like a laundry detergent? They might say that it is the new and improved version of the old laundry detergent, and the implication is that one is to no longer use the old version. This is the meaning of the term "New Testament" in relationship to the "Old Testament," that the "old" has been replaced by the "new." The term "testament" means "agreement," or "contract," or "covenant." When Christians use the term "New Testament," it is a way of saying the new covenant that they feel exists between God and believing Christians, has replaced the old contract, or old covenant, the old testament, between God and the Jews.

For this reason, Jews who respect their own faith and their own Hebrew Scriptures should never refer to their own Scriptures as the "Old Testament." The reason is that the term is insulting to Judaism and to Jews. We don't believe in a New Testament, and so we certainly should not call ours, the "Old Testament."

As we said, the first verse of Jeremiah 31:31 speaks of a "new covenant:"

> *Behold, the days come, saith the Eternal, that I will make a new covenant with the house of Israel, and with the house of Judah*

But one could ask the question, "is this new covenant a covenant which replaces any of the covenants that God made with the Jews beforehand?"

When God makes a new covenant with the Jews, it is only to re-establish and re-affirm the covenants with the Jews that came before. The covenant God made with Isaac did not replace or break the covenant God made with Abraham. The covenant that God made with Jacob did not replace or break the covenant God made with Isaac or with Abraham. One example of this can be seen in Leviticus 26:42, where the Jews were told in the verses just before verse 42 that when they sin, they will be punished for their sins, but then they are told that God's covenant with them is eternal:

> *Then will I remember my covenant with Jacob, and also my covenant with Isaac, and also my covenant with Abraham will I remember; and I will remember the land.*

Had the covenants that God made with Isaac and Abraham been made null and void by the covenant God made with Jacob, there would have been no need to have specified the covenants God had made with Isaac and Abraham in the verse above.

The covenant that God made with the People of Israel through Moses, did not replace or break the covenant God made with Jacob, or with Isaac, or with Abraham. Every subsequent covenant that God makes with the Jews, re-affirms and re-establishes the covenant that God made with the Jews before it.

The covenant that God made with the Jews is an eternal covenant, and it is a covenant made with them, with their descendants, and with all those who convert to Judaism. God's promise to the Jews, that His covenant with them is eternal, is repeated over and over again throughout the Hebrew Scriptures. Here are just a few examples:

> Genesis 17:7-8 *And I will establish my covenant between me and thee and thy seed after thee in their generations for an everlasting covenant, to be a God unto*

thee, and to thy seed after thee. 8 And I will give unto thee, and to thy seed after thee, the land wherein thou art a stranger, all the land of Canaan, for an everlasting possession; and I will be their God.

See also Genesis 17:12-13, Genesis 17:19

Psalm 105:6-10 O ye seed of Abraham His servant, ye children of Jacob His chosen. 7 He is the Eternal our God: His judgments are in all the earth. 8 He hath remembered His covenant for ever, the word which He commanded to a thousand generations. 9 Which covenant He made with Abraham, and His oath unto Isaac; 10 And confirmed the same unto Jacob for a law, and to Israel for an everlasting covenant:

The above verses from Psalm 105 are also found in I Chronicles 16:13-17.

More importantly, that the covenant between God and the Jews is eternal is also found immediately following the very passage in question, of Jeremiah 31:31-34, beginning with the very next verse:

35 Thus saith the Eternal, which giveth the sun for a light by day, and the ordinances of the moon and of the stars for a light by night, which divideth the sea when the waves thereof roar; The Eternal of hosts is his name: 36 If those ordinances depart from before me, saith the Eternal, then the seed of Israel also shall cease from being a nation before me for ever.

If ever the sun and the moon and the stars, as well as the sea and the waves ever ceased to exist and stopped following the laws governing them, then, of course, the People of Israel would not exist, because all of life would no longer exist, and only then would the covenant between God and the Jews also cease to exist.

So the covenant between God and the Jews is an eternal covenant, and when God makes a new covenant, it is with the Jews and it only re-affirms and re-establishes the earlier covenants which God had made with the Jews, as we saw regarding Leviticus 26:42 above.

Again, let us look at the first verse of our passage from Jeremiah 31:31-34:

> *31 Behold, the days come, saith the Eternal, that I will make a new covenant with the house of Israel, and with the house of Judah*

This is considered a prophecy because of the first words of the verse, *'Behold, the days come, saith the Eternal.'* However, immediately before these few verses that begin with verse 31, there are additional verses that also begin the exact same way, with the words, *"Behold, the days come, saith the Eternal."* When Christians refer to Jeremiah 31:31-34, they are leaving out half of the prophecy because the whole prophecy actually begins with verse 27. As you will read, when one looks at the whole prophecy of Jeremiah 31:27-34, this passage could not be referring to Christianity at all. Here is the whole passage:

> *27 Behold, the days come, saith the Eternal, that I will sow the house of Israel and the house of Judah with the seed of man, and with the seed of beast. 28 And it shall come to pass, that like as I have watched over them, to pluck up, and to break down, and to throw down, and to destroy, and to afflict; so will I watch over them, to build, and to plant, saith the Eternal. 29 In those days they shall say no more, The fathers have eaten a sour grape, and the children's teeth are set on edge. 30 But every one shall die for his own iniquity: every man that eateth the sour grape, his teeth shall be set on edge. 31 Behold, the days come, saith the Eternal, that I will make a new covenant with the house of Israel, and with the house of Judah: 32 Not*

according to the covenant that I made with their fathers in the day that I took them by the hand to bring them out of the land of Egypt; which my covenant they brake, although I was an husband unto them, saith the Eternal: 33 But this shall be the covenant that I will make with the house of Israel; After those days, saith the Eternal, I will put my law in their inward parts, and write it in their hearts; and will be their God, and they shall be my people. 34 And they shall teach no more every man his neighbour, and every man his brother, saying, Know the Eternal: for they shall all know me, from the least of them unto the greatest of them, saith the Eternal: for I will forgive their iniquity, and I will remember their sin no more.

These verses are, indeed, speaking of the Messianic age; however, they are not speaking of the coming of Jesus and Christianity.

Verse 27 speaks of a time when the House of Israel is reunited with the House of Judah, and when they increase in size as well as in resources.

27 Behold, the days come, saith the Eternal, that I will sow the house of Israel and the house of Judah with the seed of man, and with the seed of beast.

Then God states that just as He watched over the Jews when He saw fit to punish them, so, too, will He continue to watch over the Jews as everything gets better:

28 And it shall come to pass, that like as I have watched over them, to pluck up, and to break down, and to throw down, and to destroy, and to afflict; so will I watch over them, to build, and to plant, saith the Eternal.

The next verses actually deny the most basic belief of Christianity, that Jesus can die for your sins:

> *29 In those days they shall say no more, The fathers have eaten a sour grape, and the children's teeth are set on edge. 30 But every one shall die for his own iniquity: every man that eateth the sour grape, his teeth shall be set on edge.*

Verses 29-30 above are saying that in this future time, no one will continue to believe that one person can die and thereby take away the guilt for another person's sins. This is shown by those who recite an old saying (also found in Ezekiel 18) that the father eats sour grapes, but that it is the children who taste the sourness. This old saying expressed the erroneous belief that the parents would sin, but that it was the children who inherited the guilt of their parents' sins. Instead, Jeremiah is saying that when those days come, all will recognize, as the Bible has said repeatedly (See Exodus 32:30-35; Deuteronomy 24:16; and Ezekiel 18:1-4) that the person who sins will always be the only one who gets the punishment for that sin. Of course, this means that Jesus cannot die for your sin! This is what it states quite simply in Deuteronomy 24:16, *"No man shall be put to death for the sins of his children; no child will be put to death for the sins of his father. Every man shall be put to death for his own sin."*

This description of this messianic age continues with Jeremiah 31:31, which is the passage that Christians usually quote without the verses that come before it. Just a simple overview of these verses indicates that what it describes has not happened yet.

The first verse of the passage reads,

> *31 'Behold, the days come, saith the Eternal, that I will make a new covenant with the house of Israel, and with the house of Judah.'*

However, the House of Israel, which was made up of the Ten Lost Tribes, have been lost and scattered around the world since the fall of the Northern Kingdom around 721 B.C.E. The House of Israel, the Ten Lost Tribes, cannot be re-united with the House of Jacob, because the House of Israel has not been around for thousands of years. That is why they are called the Ten *Lost* Tribes.

This passage in Jeremiah is describing a Jewish People where all of the descendants of every tribe thrive, and made their way to the Promised Land. Because it speaks of both the House of Israel and the House of Judah together, with God, in a single new covenant, and since the House of Israel cannot be unified with the House of Judah, this entire passage has not happened yet, and cannot refer to Christianity or their "new covenant."

There is another reference, also in Jeremiah, in the 23rd chapter, that describes the same thing, where all the Jews have returned to the Promised Land, and which also begins with the same words found in Jeremiah 31:27 and 31:31

> Jeremiah 23:5-8 *5 Behold, the days come, saith the Eternal, that I will raise unto David a righteous Branch, and a King shall reign and prosper, and shall execute judgment and justice in the earth. 6 In his days Judah shall be saved, and Israel shall dwell safely: and this is his name whereby he shall be called, The Eternal Is Our Righteousness. 7 Therefore, behold, the days come, saith the Eternal, that they shall no more say, The Eternal liveth, which brought up the children of Israel out of the land of Egypt; 8 But, The Eternal liveth, which brought up and which led the seed of the House of Israel out of the north country, and from all countries whither I had driven them; and they shall dwell in their own land.*

This leads us, now, to look at the next two verses of our passage:

> *32 Not according to the covenant that I made with their fathers in the day that I took them by the hand to bring them out of the land of Egypt; which my covenant they broke, although I was a husband unto them, saith the Eternal: 33 But this shall be the covenant that I will make with the house of Israel; After those days, saith the Eternal, I will put my Torah in their inward parts, and write it in their hearts; and will be their God, and they shall be my people.*

What these verses are saying is that everyone will no longer need to look in any book, neither a New Testament, nor even the Hebrew Scriptures, to tell them what is Right and what is Wrong. They will know it instinctively because it will be in their hearts, truly making God their God, and in turn, truly making them God's People. Certainly this has also not happened yet, and so this passage cannot be referring to Christianity, nor can it be referring to their New Testament.

What, precisely, does it mean to have God's Torah written in our innermost parts? Psalm 40:8 says,:

> *I delight to do thy will, O my God: yea, thy Torah is within my heart.*

Because God's Torah is within us, we know what we are to do, and we are happy to do it.

Please also read carefully. Jeremiah 31:33 does not say "I will put my NEW Torah in their inward parts . . ." It says, "I will put my Torah in their inward parts." It remains the same Torah as before. The laws of God do not change or get changed, they are eternal as God is Eternal:

> Deuteronomy 29:29 *The secret things belong unto the Eternal our God: but those things which are revealed belong unto us and to our children for ever, that we may do all the words of this Torah.*

> Psalm 19:7-9 *7 The Torah of the Eternal is perfect, converting the soul: the testimony of the Eternal is sure, making wise the simple. 8 The statutes of the Eternal are right, rejoicing the heart: the commandment of the Eternal is pure, enlightening the eyes. 9 The fear of the Eternal is clean, enduring for ever: the judgments of the Eternal are true and righteous altogether.*

Psalm 111:7-8 *7 The works of his hands are verity and judgment; all his commandments are sure. 8 They stand fast for ever and ever, and are done in truth and uprightness.*

As a matter of fact, Ezekiel 11:17-20 reflects the ideas found in Jeremiah 31:27-34 that God's laws will be in our hearts, not books, in the messianic age, which will last forever:

Ezekiel 11:17-20 *17 Therefore say, Thus saith the Eternal God; I will even gather you from the people, and assemble you out of the countries where ye have been scattered, and I will give you the land of Israel. 18 And they shall come thither, and they shall take away all the detestable things thereof and all the abominations thereof from thence. 19 And I will give them one heart, and I will put a new spirit within you; and I will take the stony heart out of their flesh, and will give them an heart of flesh: 20 That they may walk in my statutes, and keep mine ordinances, and do them: and they shall be my people, and I will be their God.*

As I wrote above, this new covenant that God speaks about in Jeremiah 31 is not talking about a new covenant, a new contract, with a new people, and He does not mean a new set of laws, a new Torah, a new scripture. It means the covenant between God and the Jews and the laws of that covenant are eternal.

Finally, the text From Jeremiah 31 reads,

34 And they shall teach no more every man his neighbour, and every man his brother, saying, Know the Eternal: for they shall all know me, from the least of them unto the greatest of them, saith the Eternal: for I will forgive their iniquity, and I will remember their sin no more.

This new covenant means that no one will have to missionize anyone to "Know the Eternal," because the whole world will already believe in God. This part of the passage especially has not happened yet, and this is proven because had it already happened, then Christianity would have no need to missionize anyone! Since they spend hundreds of millions of dollars every year, just to missionize the Jews, just to get the Jews to "Know the Lord," then this prophecy in Jeremiah 31 has not happened yet, and these Christian missionaries prove it every day.

8. Psalm 110:1

Another verse that Christian missionaries are fond of quoting in order to convert Jews to their faith is Psalm 110:1. In Christian translations, this verse reads,

> *A Psalm of David. The Lord said unto my Lord, Sit thou at my right hand, until I make thine enemies thy footstool.*

Christians see this verse as a statement that God, referred to in the first use of the word "Lord," was speaking to Jesus, referred to in the second use of the word, "Lord." Christians understand this verse to be saying, "God said to Jesus . . ." Of course, this leads me to ask the question, if Jesus were God, than why would God the Father have to make Jesus' enemies into Jesus' footstool? If Jesus were God, he would be able to do that on his own?

Be that as it may, there are other great problems with this verse. There are no capital letters in Hebrew. By capitalizing both instances of the word "Lord," in the English translation, it makes it seem as though both words refer to deity, or to someone who is divine. It is a way of leading the reader to view this verse as one divine entity speaking to another divine entity, which is an interpretation in and of itself because they are choosing to capitalize the first letter of the word in both uses of the word "Lord."

To really understand this verse, or for that matter any verse from the Hebrew Scriptures, one must read it in the original Hebrew. This verse begins, in transliteration:

"L'David mizmor. Ne'um Y.H.V.H. L'Adonee . . ."

There are numerous ways to translate the first phrase of this verse, "L'David mizmor." The reason is that the prefix of "L" can mean "of," or "for," or "to." This means that there are three possible translations of this phrase, and each one is possibly correct. They are "Of David," or "For David," or "To David."

If the correct translation is "Of David," then it would mean that David wrote this psalm. However, if the correct translation is "To David," or "For David," then it would mean that this was written by someone other than King David, the author is unknown, and this unknown author dedicated it *to* King David, or he wrote it *for* King David.

The first word used in the verse that is translated as "Lord," is, indeed, the holiest name for God, called the "tetragrammaton," which means "the four lettered name." However, the second word that is translated as "Lord" is not the four letter name for God, the tetragrammaton, but rather it is the word "Adonee," which means "my master," or "my lord" as in the "lords and ladies" of England's nobility. This is the way that the authors of the King James translation would have understood it. The better way to translate this phrase, then, would be "God said to my master," and would have been written by a Psalmist other than King David, about King David, and for King David. Another way to understand this verse would be to read it as if it said, "God said to King David."

This verse was written about King David, for King David, and the author is saying that God was going to make King David's enemies into King David's footstool, meaning that King David was going to walk all over his enemies, and, indeed, this is what happened. King David defeated the Philistines, and he forced the Moabites to pay him tribute.

Although Christians wish to see this verse as a proof text for their Christian theology, it is interesting the way in which Jesus uses this verse in their own New Testament. Jesus quotes this verse to prove that the messiah was not going to be a descendant of King David, in spite of the fact that Judaism and the Jewish people have always believed that the messiah had to be a descendant of King David.

In the verses below, Jesus quotes this verse from Psalm 110:1, and also sees this as King David writing about how God spoke to the messiah. However, Jesus asks how can the messiah be the descendant of King David, if King David himself refers to the messiah as King David's Lord?

> Matthew 22:41-46 *While the Pharisees were gathered together, Jesus asked them, 42 Saying, What think ye of Christ? Whose son is he? They say unto him, The Son of David. 43 He saith unto them, How then doth David in spirit call him Lord, saying, 44 The Lord said unto my Lord, Sit thou on my right hand, till I make thine enemies thy footstool? 45 If David then call him Lord, how is he his son? 46 And no man was able to answer him a word, neither durst any man from that day forth ask him any more questions.*

Christian missionaries wish to view Psalm 110 as though it proves that the messiah will be God, but Jesus, in the Christian's New Testament, uses the very same verse to prove that the messiah, if he is divine, cannot be a descendant of King David. Jesus, according to Christian theology was, himself, a descendant of King David, so, according to Jesus in the above verses, Jesus could not have been the messiah. Christians cannot have it both ways.

9. Proverbs 30:2-4

Christian missionaries will show Jews the following verses, and ask them to answer the question at the end of verse 4:

> Proverbs 30:2 *Surely I am more brutish than any man, and have not the understanding of a man. 3 I neither learned wisdom, nor have the knowledge of the holy. 4 Who hath*

ascended up into heaven, or descended? who hath gathered the wind in his fists? who hath bound the waters in a garment? who hath established all the ends of the earth? what is his name, and what is his son's name, if thou canst tell?

Because the verse ends with the questions, '*What is his name and what is his son's name, if thou canst tell?*' then Christians will tell you that this is a reference to Jesus, the son of God, who, because he was God, can do all the things listed in these verses. Of course, this interpretation can only be valid for those who assume that Jesus was God.

This is not the Jewish interpretation of these verses. These verses are asking rhetorical questions. The Psalmist knows that no one, other than God, can *"gather the wind in his fists, bound the waters in a garment, or establish all the ends of the earth."* These verses are saying that there is no one other than God who can do these things, by asking "who can do these things" in a rhetorical way. The Bible is clear, only God controls nature, and only God is the author of Creation. Since the answer is that it is beyond human capability, there is no human being who can do it. Since there is no human who can do it, there is no name of this non-existent person, and there is no son to this non-existent person, either. This verse is a rhetorical way of saying, simply, there is no one like God.

Furthermore, in the Bible there are many who were called the son of God. One example is the Jewish people.

In the following verses, God is telling Moses what to tell Pharaoh. And here, God explicitly states that the People of Israel, the Jews, are God's firstborn son:

Exodus 4:21-23 *And the Eternal said unto Moses, When thou goest to return into Egypt, see that thou do all those wonders before Pharaoh, which I have put in thine hand: but I will harden his heart, that he shall not let the people go. 22 And thou shalt say unto Pharaoh, Thus saith the Eternal, Israel is my son, even my firstborn: 23 And I say unto thee, Let my son go, that he may serve me: and if thou refuse to let him go, behold, I will slay thy son, even thy firstborn.*

As I wrote in the beginning, there are other interpretations that are possible. Perhaps the son of God that Proverbs 30:4 is speaking of is King David, because we have the following Biblical verses in Psalm 89:20-27 that say exactly that:

> 20 I have found David my servant; with my holy oil have I anointed him: 21 With whom my hand shall be established: mine arm also shall strengthen him. 22 The enemy shall not exact upon him; nor the son of wickedness afflict him. 23 And I will beat down his foes before his face, and plague them that hate him. 24 But my faithfulness and my mercy shall be with him: and in my name shall his horn be exalted. 25 I will set his hand also in the sea, and his right hand in the rivers. 26 He shall cry unto me, Thou art my father, my God, and the rock of my salvation. 27 Also I will make him my firstborn, higher than the kings of the earth.

Or, perhaps, Psalm 30:4 is referring to King Solomon, whom God also calls His son, in I Chronicles 22:9-10:

> Behold, a son shall be born to thee, who shall be a man of rest; and I will give him rest from all his enemies round about: for his name shall be Solomon and I will give peace and quietness unto Israel in his days. 10 He shall build an house for my name; and he shall be my son, and I will be his father; and I will establish the throne of his kingdom over Israel for ever.

So there are a few interpretations of this Proverb, however they do not require us to interpret it in a way that is contrary to the Bible.

10. Isaiah 53

To missionary Christians, Isaiah 53 is the perfect description of the life and death of Jesus. Because it is so perfect a description, they feel that Jesus must have been the Messiah because he seems to have fulfilled the prophecy of Isaiah 53.

Some of these Fundamentalist Christians are told that this is so perfect a description of Jesus that the Jews are forbidden to read it! Furthermore, they are told that the Jews read from the Prophets every week in their religious services, but the 53rd chapter of Isaiah was intentionally left out of those readings because it is so obviously a description of Jesus.

No part of the Jewish Bible was ever censored by the Jewish people; at no time were Jews forbidden to read certain parts of the Bible. Had the Jews wanted to censor any part of the Bible, they simply would have removed it from the bible to begin with, or not included it in the Canon. It was, after all, the Jews, specifically the Rabbis of the post second-Temple period that determined what would, and what would not, be in the Bible.

Of course, it is a matter of history that Christians were not allowed to read the Bible on their own. Translators of the Bible were killed by the Church because it made the Bible accessible to the common people.

The portion from the Prophets, called the Haftarah, is read only because there was a certain time in Jewish history when they were forbidden by non-Jews to read from the Torah on pain of death. In order to let the Jews know what should have been read from the Torah, sections of the Prophets and the Writings were chosen to be read which were parallel to the Torah portion it replaced. After the Jews were once again allowed to read from the Torah, the custom of reading the Haftarah remained because it enhanced the meaning of the Torah. The reason that Jews do not read Isaiah 53 at any time of the year during a weekly service is because there are no parallels to Isaiah 53 in the Torah, the Five Books of Moses, Genesis, Exodus, Leviticus, Numbers, and Deuteronomy.

An example of this can be shown from the Haftarah reading for Genesis 1:1, the Creation story. For this Sabbath, the parallel reading from the Prophets is Isaiah 42:5-43:11, which begins, "Thus says God, the Lord, Who created the Heavens and stretched them out . . . ."

Isaiah 53 does not parallel anything in the Torah, and therefore it was not chosen to be read in place of anything in the Torah.

The only reason Christians are told that the Jews are forbidden to read Isaiah 53, or that the Jews do not read Isaiah 53 when they read from the Prophets, is because they cannot understand how the Jews can read Isaiah 53 and not immediately admit that Jesus was its fulfillment and therefore the Messiah. Of course, as we shall see, there are quite a few reasons why the Jews do not view the prophecy of Isaiah 53 was fulfilled in Jesus.

Despite what we have just stated, as you read the text of Isaiah 53, you may indeed see within the verses what seems to be a description of Jesus. There is a reason for this which we shall discuss below.

Please remember that this is, indeed, a *mistranslation* of the original Hebrew, however, we will use it because it is the *mistranslation* most often used by Christian missionaries:

> Isaiah 52:13-53:12 *13 Behold, my servant shall deal prudently, he shall be exalted and extolled, and be very high. 14 As many were astonished at thee; his visage was so marred more than any man, and his form more than the sons of men: 15 So shall he sprinkle many nations; the kings shall shut their mouths at him: for that which had not been told them shall they see; and that which they had not heard shall they consider.*

> Isaiah 53:1 *1 Who hath believed our report? and to whom is the arm of the Eternal revealed? 2 For he shall grow up before him as a tender plant, and as a root out of a dry ground: he hath no form nor comeliness; and when we shall see him, there is no beauty that we should desire him. 3 He is despised and rejected of men; a man of sorrows, and acquainted with grief: and we hid as it were our faces from him; he was despised, and we esteemed him not. 4 Surely he hath borne our griefs, and carried our sorrows: yet we did esteem him stricken, smitten of God, and afflicted. 5*

> *But he was wounded for our transgressions, he was bruised for our iniquities: the chastisement of our peace was upon him; and with his stripes we are healed. 6 All we like sheep have gone astray; we have turned every one to his own way; and the Eternal hath laid on him the iniquity of us all. 7 He was oppressed, and he was afflicted, yet he opened not his mouth: he is brought as a lamb to the slaughter, and as a sheep before her shearers is dumb, so he openeth not his mouth. 8 He was taken from prison and from judgment: and who shall declare his generation? for he was cut off out of the land of the living: for the transgression of my people was he stricken. 9 And he made his grave with the wicked, and with the rich in his death; because he had done no violence, neither was any deceit in his mouth. 10 Yet it pleased the Eternal to bruise him; he hath put him to grief: when thou shalt make his soul an offering for sin, he shall see his seed, he shall prolong his days, and the pleasure of the Eternal shall prosper in his hand. 11 He shall see of the travail of his soul, and shall be satisfied: by his knowledge shall my righteous servant justify many; for he shall bear their iniquities. 12 Therefore will I divide him a portion with the great, and he shall divide the spoil with the strong; because he hath poured out his soul unto death: and he was numbered with the transgressors; and he bare the sin of many, and made intercession for the transgressors.*

First, let me point out just two of the many mistranslations in the above. In verse 5, the text is translated as, *"But he was wounded FOR our transgressions, he was bruised FOR our iniquities . . . ."* The mistake is that the prefix to the Hebrew words meaning, "our transgressions" and "our iniquities" is the Hebrew letter, mem. This is a prefix meaning "from" and not "for." A more accurate translation would be, "But he was wounded FROM our transgressions, he was bruised FROM our iniquities." This means that Isaiah 53 is not talking about a man who died "for our sins," but rather it is about a man who died "BECAUSE of our sins." This, indeed, is the Jewish understanding of Isaiah 53, that the nations of the earth will finally understand that the Jews have been right all along, and that the sins committed against the Jews by the nations of the earth resulted in the death of innocent Jews.

In verse 9, the text above is translated as, *"And they made his grave with the wicked and with a rich man in his death."* However, this last word in the Hebrew is more accurately translated as "in his deaths," because the word appears in the Hebrew in the plural. The text reads, "b'mo-taYv." The Hebrew letter "Yod" indicated by the capital Y in the transliterated word, indicates the plural, as anyone who knows Hebrew would understand. To read, "in his death," the text would have to read "b'moto." Since the word "b'mo-taYv" actually means "in his deaths," then for Jesus to fulfill this verse, he must therefore come back to earth and die at least another time. The Jews, personified as the servant as we shall see below, have fulfilled this verse time and time again, because the People of Israel have had countless millions die undeserved deaths.

As you have read the above verses, you may have been reminded of the image of Jesus, how he lived and how he died. If this is so, then why isn't Isaiah 53 a prophecy concerning the Messiah which Jesus fulfilled, according to the Jewish understanding of this passage?

According to Jewish tradition, Isaiah was writing about the People of Israel personified as The Suffering Servant of the Lord. And there are no less than eight quotations that show this to be true. Please note that in the following quotations, all from the Book of Isaiah, it is the People of Israel who are called the Servant of the Lord. The name, "Israel," is another name for Jacob, and so when the text reads "Jacob" or "Israel," it means the same people.

Isaiah 41:8 *But you, Israel, my servant, Jacob, whom I have chosen, the offspring of Abraham, my friend.*

Isaiah 43:10 *Ye are my witnesses, saith the Eternal, and my servant whom I have chosen: that ye may know and believe me, and understand that I am he: before me there was no God formed, neither shall there be after me.*

Isaiah 44:1 *Yet now hear, O Jacob my servant; and Israel, whom I have chosen:*

Isaiah 44:21 *Remember these things, O Jacob, and Israel, for you are my servant; I formed you, you are my servant; O Israel, you will not be forgotten by me.*

Isaiah 45:4 *For the sake of my servant Jacob, and Israel my chosen, I call you by your name, I surname you, though you do not know me.*

Isaiah 48:20 *Go ye forth of Babylon, flee ye from the Chaldeans, with a voice of singing declare ye, tell this, utter it even to the end of the earth; say ye, The Eternal hath redeemed his servant Jacob.*

Isaiah 49:3 *And He said to me, 'You are my servant, Israel, in whom I will be glorified.*

Isaiah 49:7 *Thus saith the Eternal, the Redeemer of Israel, and his Holy One, to him whom man despiseth, to him whom the nation abhorreth, to a servant of rulers, Kings shall see and arise, princes also shall worship, because of the Eternal that is faithful, and the Holy One of Israel, and he shall choose thee.*

Above, Isaiah 43:10 is a very interesting verse. That verse tells us that the Jewish People are plural, when God uses the term "witnesses," but the People of Israel are also referred to in this same verse in the singular in the word, "servant," the same word that we find in Isaiah 53!

This verse also states that there will be "no God formed," which means that Jesus cannot be God, who was formed in Mary's womb well after God spoke these words in Isaiah 43:10.

From the many above quotations we can see that Isaiah 53 was referring to the People of Israel as a Suffering Servant of the Eternal, just as in all of the quotations which came before Isaiah 53.

Christian missionaries will claim that Rashi, which is an acronym for Rabbi Shlomo Yitzchaki (1040-1105), made up the association of the Suffering Servant of Isaiah 53 with the People of Israel personified. This is simply wrong, which can be proven from the writings of Christians themselves well before Rashi was born. In "Contra Celsum," written in 248 C.E. (some 800 years before Rashi), the Christian Church Father Origen records that Jews living in his time period interpreted this passage as referring to the entire nation of Israel. He wrote:

"I remember that once in a discussion with some whom the Jews regard as learned I used these prophecies [Isaiah 52:13-53:8]. At this the Jew said that these prophecies referred to the whole people as though of a single individual, since they were scattered in the dispersion and smitten, that as a result of the scattering of the Jews among the other nations many might become proselytes." (Origen, Contra Celsum, trans. Henry Chadwick, Cambridge: Cambridge University Press, Book 1.55, 1965, p. 50. This can also be found on the internet at:

http://www.ccel.org/ccel/schaff/anf04.vi.ix.i.lvi.html)

This shows that Jews subscribed to the belief that the people of Israel were the suffering servant spoken of throughout the entire passage, and this pre-dates Rashi by many centuries.

Before we look directly at Isaiah 53, we must first ask a question. The Bible is explicitly clear, as we read in Deuteronomy 24:16, that "Every one is to be put to death for his own sin." This is also found in Exodus 32:30-35 "And the Eternal said unto Moses, Whosoever hath sinned against me, him will I blot out of my book," and again in Ezekiel 18:1-4; 20-24; 26-27 "Behold, all souls are mine; as the soul of the father, so also the soul of the son is mine: the soul that sinneth, it shall die . . . 20 The soul that sinneth, it shall die. The son shall not bear the iniquity of the father, neither shall the father bear the iniquity of the son: the righteousness of the righteous shall be upon him, and the wickedness of the wicked shall be upon him." Please note that in Ezekiel 18:20 it does not say that the wickedness of the wicked shall be upon the righteous, but rather the wickedness of the wicked shall be upon the wicked.

As I have shown above, the Bible repeatedly, consistently, and without any need of interpretation, literally and clearly states that the person who sins is the person who gets the punishment for the sin. The question we must ask in light of the Christian interpretation of Isaiah 53 is, "When did God change His mind?" If, indeed, "every man is to be put to death for his own sin," then the only way one can interpret Isaiah 53 to mean the opposite, that Jesus died for your sins, is if God changed His mind. Otherwise, He did not mean what He said when He said, "every man is to be put to death for his own sin." The interpretation Christians give to Isaiah 53 is exactly that, an interpretation, and one that goes against the ideas expressed elsewhere in the Bible as we have shown.

This Christian interpretation of a dying/saving messiah is also one that was unknown to Jesus' disciples, as we have mentioned at the end of Chapter 6 of this book. When Jesus explained his mission to his disciples, that he was to die for the sins of humanity according to this definition of "messiah," his disciples did not understand what he was saying, and their response was to rebuke Jesus for having said it, according to Matthew 16:13-23:

> *13 When Jesus came into the coasts of Caesarea Philippi, he asked his disciples, saying, Whom do men say that I the Son of man am? 14 And they said, Some say that thou art John the Baptist: some, Elias; and others, Jeremias, or one of the prophets. 15 He saith unto them, But whom say ye that I am? 16 And Simon Peter answered and said, Thou art the Christ, the Son of the living God. 17 And Jesus answered and said unto him, Blessed art thou, Simon Barjona: for flesh and blood hath not revealed it unto thee, but my Father which is in heaven . . . . 20 Then charged he his disciples that they should tell no man that he was Jesus*

the Christ. 21 From that time forth began Jesus to shew unto his disciples, how that he must go unto Jerusalem, and suffer many things of the elders and chief priests and scribes, and be killed, and be raised again the third day. 22 Then Peter took him, and began to rebuke him, saying, Be it far from thee, Lord: this shall not be unto thee. 23 But he turned, and said unto Peter, Get thee behind me, Satan: thou art an offence unto me: for thou savourest not the things that be of God, but those that be of men.

See also, Mark 8:31-33, and Luke 18:31-34. Had Peter and the other disciples known about the dying/saving mission of the messiah, they would have thanked Jesus rather than rebuked him for what he told them.

Read the passage from Isaiah 52:13 to Isaiah 53:12 again. Certainly, if one does not read carefully, it does sound a lot like a description of a man who dies for the sins of others. This is similar to the story of Pinocchio, as we discussed in the Introduction to Section II, under Typologies. How do Jews explain that the life and death of Jesus is reflected in these verses?

First of all, it should not surprise you that the life and death of Jesus seems to be reflected within the verses of Isaiah 53. The Hebrew Scriptures came before Jesus. The authors of the Christian's New Testament could use images they found in the Hebrew Scriptures and create a story about Jesus to fit those images, as we have already discussed in the Introduction, in Section C Inventions.

Many of the passages in the Christian's New Testament contradict the image described in Isaiah 53. This is probably because no matter how hard the authors tried to create stories about Jesus that would fit images found in the Hebrew Scriptures, the factual stories about the man Jesus were also recorded by them. These are the stories that deny any Messiah-ship of Jesus, as well as contradict the image of the Suffering Servant in Isaiah 53. Let us take a closer look at what Isaiah 53 says, and then compare it with other passages from the Christian's New Testament.

Two verses in the Isaiah passage describe the servant of the Lord as having been either too ugly to be human in appearance, or too plain-looking to make us notice him:

> Isaiah 52:14 *His appearance was so marred, beyond human semblance, and his form beyond that of the sons of men.*

> Isaiah 53:2 *He had no form or comeliness that we should look at him, and no beauty that we should desire him.*

But every single picture painted of Jesus shows a man who was both handsome and tall and generally muscular, as any carpenter would be. These texts from Isaiah are not referring to The Servant at only a single time and place, like after a scourging, or crucifixion, but rather it refers to the way The Servant looks, in general, to the non-Jewish world.

There is also evidence in the Christian's New Testament that indicates that Jesus was a handsome man, whose company was desired by others, and whose stature, or appearance, does not match Isaiah's description:

> Luke 2:52 *And Jesus increased in wisdom and in stature, and in favor with God and man.*

One verse in the Isaiah passage describes the servant as a loner, without anyone to call a friend:

> Isaiah 53:3 *He was despised and rejected by men.*

The above verse is not describing a man who, at one point in his life, has some who rejected him, but rather one who has known rejection throughout his life as the Jews have known throughout our 4,000 years of existence. However, in many places within the Christian's New Testament, like the above quotation from Luke 2:52,

Jesus is described as having a huge following, from the beginning of his ministry all the way to the scene at the crucifixion:

> Matthew 21:46 *But when they tried to arrest him, they feared the multitudes, because they held him to be a prophet.*

> Luke 23:26-27 *And as they led him away, they seized one Simon of Cyrene, who was coming in from the country, and laid on him the cross, to carry it behind Jesus. 27 And there followed him a great multitude of the people, and of women who bewailed and lamented him.*

This can also be seen in the following verses:

> Mark 14:1-2 *After two days was the feast of the Passover, and of unleavened bread: and the chief priests and the scribes sought how they might take him by craft, and put him to death. 2 But they said, Not on the feast day, lest there be an uproar of the people.*

> Matthew 4:24-25 *And his fame went throughout all Syria: and they brought unto him all sick people that were taken with diverse diseases and torments, and those which were possessed with devils, and those which were lunatic, and those that had the palsy; and he healed them. 25 And there followed him great multitudes of people from Galilee, and from Decapolis, and from Jerusalem, and from Judaea, and from beyond Jordan.*

> Matthew 21:9 *And the multitudes that went before, and that followed, cried, saying, Hosanna to the Son of David: Blessed is he that cometh in the name of the Lord; Hosanna in the highest.*

Matthew 21:11 *And the multitude said, This is Jesus the prophet of Nazareth of Galilee.*

Luke 4:14-15 *And Jesus returned in the power of the Spirit into Galilee: and there went out a fame of him through all the region round about. 15 And he taught in their synagogues, being glorified of all.*

Luke 7:11-12 *And it came to pass the day after, that he went into a city called Nain; and many of his disciples went with him, and much people. 12 Now when he came nigh to the gate of the city, behold, there was a dead man carried out, the only son of his mother, and she was a widow: and much people of the city was with her.*

Luke 7:16-17 *And there came a fear on all: and they glorified God, saying, That a great prophet is risen up among us; and, That God hath visited his people. 17 And this rumour of him went forth throughout all Judaea, and throughout all the region round about.*

Luke 8:4 *And when much people were gathered together, and were come to him out of every city, he spake by a parable:*

Luke 8:19 *Then came to him his mother and his brethren, and could not come at him for the press.*

Luke 8:45 *And Jesus said, Who touched me? When all denied, Peter and they that were with him said, Master, the multitude throng thee and press thee, and sayest thou, Who touched me?*

John 12:11 *Because that by reason of him many of the Jews went away, and believed on Jesus.*

> John 12:42 *Nevertheless among the chief rulers also many believed on him; but because of the Pharisees they did not confess him, lest they should be put out of the synagogue:*

So we see that unlike the servant described in Isaiah 53:3, Jesus was neither despised nor rejected by all men, and instead, he maintained a large following even up until he was crucified.

Two quotations from the Isaiah passage describe someone who remains silent when accused by his captors, one who is innocent of any wrongdoing:

> Isaiah 53:7 *like a lamb that is led to the slaughter, and like a sheep that before its shearers is dumb, so he opened not his mouth.*

> Isaiah 53:9 *and there was no deceit in his mouth.*

But there is one quotation in the Christian's New Testament that states that Jesus did rebuke his captors and in so doing did in fact "open his mouth."

> John 18:22-23 *And when he had thus spoken, one of the officers which stood by struck Jesus with the palm of his hand, saying, Answerest thou the high priest so? 23 Jesus answered him, If I have spoken evil, bear witness of the evil: but if well, why smitest thou me?*

In the above quotation, Jesus rebukes his captors for what he considers mistreatment. As we have discussed elsewhere, Jesus demanded an explanation of why he had been struck. In "opening up his mouth" to rebuke his captors, he contradicts his own idea of "turning the other cheek," found in Matthew 5:39. This makes Jesus a hypocrite, and hypocrisy is a form of deceit because it deceives people in to doing what the deceiver himself does not do.

One of the verses in the Isaiah passage describes an innocent man of peace:

Isaiah 53:9 *although he had done no violence*

But most people are familiar with at least one of the many acts of violence that Jesus did, which was the "cleansing" of the Temple:

Matthew 21:12 *And Jesus entered the Temple of God and drove out all who sold and bought in the Temple, and he overturned the tables of the money—changers and the seats of those who sold pigeons.*

Furthermore, in the version of this act of violence found in John 2:15, it states that Jesus made for himself a scourge or whip, with which to beat the people in the Temple:

John 2:15 *15 And when he had made a scourge of small cords, he drove them all out of the temple, and the sheep, and the oxen; and poured out the changers' money, and overthrew the tables;*

Although a Christian might say that the violence done by Jesus in the Temple might have been justified, the verse in Isaiah describes one who had done 'no violence' at all to make him deserving of the persecution he received. Jesus was seen by Rome as an insurrectionist, and that is why they crucified him. The New Testament states that the accusation placed above his head by Rome read, 'This is Jesus, the King of the Jews,' as we see in Matthew 27:37 as well as in Mark 15:26. His crime, according to the accusation for which he was crucified, was in trying to be the King of the Jews instead of the Emperor in Rome. The violence he perpetrated brought attention to him, and for that violence he was seen as an insurrectionist, and so he was crucified. Above, it was stated that the Jews were the servant of Isaiah 53. Some may argue that the Jews certainly did violence over the millennia, and that is true, but the Jews did no violence to deserve their persecutions. What violence did the Jews of Europe perpetrate to deserve the Holocaust?

Furthermore, those who "bought and sold in the Temple," were there because of God's command. In Deuteronomy 14:24-26, God told the Jews to sell the animal they wanted to sacrifice for money, take the money to Jerusalem, and then after changing the money to the local currency, to buy the same animal and sacrifice it. Therefore the money changers and sellers of sacrificial animals were supposed to be there, as commanded by God:

> Deuteronomy 14:24-26 *And if the way be too long for thee, so that thou art not able to carry it; or if the place be too far from thee, which the Eternal thy God shall choose to set his name there, when the Eternal thy God hath blessed thee: 25 Then shalt thou turn it into money, and bind up the money in thine hand, and shalt go unto the place which the Eternal thy God shall choose: 26 And thou shalt bestow that money for whatsoever thy soul lusteth after, for oxen, or for sheep, or for wine, or for strong drink, or for whatsoever thy soul desireth: and thou shalt eat there before the Eternal thy God, and thou shalt rejoice, thou, and thine household.*

There are other places in the New Testament that describes Jesus' violence. Here are a few more examples.

In Mark, Jesus condemns an innocent fruit tree to death because it did not have any figs on it for Jesus to eat, even though it was not even the fruit season:

> Mark 11:12-14, 20-21 *12 And on the morrow, when they were come from Bethany, he was hungry: 13 And seeing a fig tree afar off having leaves, he came, if haply he might find any thing thereon: and when he came to it, he found nothing but leaves; for the time of figs was not yet. 14 And Jesus answered and said unto it, No man eat fruit of thee hereafter forever. And his disciples heard it . . . . 20 And in*

*the morning, as they passed by, they saw the fig tree dried up
from the roots. 21 And Peter calling to remembrance saith
unto him, Master, behold, the fig tree which thou cursedst
is withered away.*

Jesus also stated that his purpose in coming to earth was not for
the sake of peace, as we have mentioned repeatedly:

Matthew 10:34-36 *34 Think not that I am come
to send peace on earth: I came not to send peace, but a
sword. 35 For I am come to set a man at variance against
his father, and the daughter against her mother, and the
daughter in law against her mother in law. 36 And a man's
foes shall be they of his own household.*

Jesus states in the following that those who won't accept him
should be slain. In almost all Christian interpretations of the parable
in which the following verse is found, Jesus is understood to have
been the ruler who speaks:

Luke 19:27 *27 But those mine enemies, which would
not that I should reign over them, bring hither, and slay
them before me.*

Perhaps the verse above from Luke 19 has been the Christian
justification for the slaying of so many Jews throughout the centuries,
simply because we still reject Jesus.

And in Luke 22:36, Jesus tells his disciples to go and buy swords.

So we see that here again, Jesus, a violent man, could not have
been the peace-loving servant who did "no violence," as described
in Isaiah 53.

Finally, there is one verse in the Isaiah passage which describes
the servant as living a long life and having children:

Isaiah 53:10 *he shall see his offspring, he shall prolong
his days;*

But quite obviously, Jesus was never married and had no children. He also died in his thirties, at a young age. Christians may respond by saying that Isaiah meant Jesus' disciples by the word, "offspring," or that the Christians themselves are like his children, but the word in the Hebrew is "Zerah," which means seed, and can only refer to one's blood-line descendants, his children. One can see this clearly in the following passage from Genesis 15:2-4. Abram is afraid that he has no biological heirs, the only one to inherit him is his servant, Eliezer, whom Abram calls his "ben," his son. However, God tells him that it will not be "his ben," his son, to inherit from him, but rather his seed, his "zerah."

> Genesis 15:2-4 *And Abram said, Eternal God, what*
> *wilt thou give me, seeing I go childless, and the son <ben>*
> *of my house is this Eliezer of Damascus? 3 And Abram said,*
> *Behold, to me thou hast given no seed <zerah—biological*
> *child>: and, lo, the son <ben> in my house is mine heir.*
> *4 And, behold, the word of the Eternal came unto him,*
> *saying, This shall not be thine heir; but he that shall come*
> *forth out of thine own bowels shall be thine heir.*

So again we see that Jesus did not fulfill the description of the servant in Isaiah 53 because he had no seed, which means no children, no offspring.

For the sake of argument, let us assume that Isaiah was making a prophecy of his future, rather than interpreting his past as the past-tenses of his speech indicate. In that case, Isaiah 53 could be applied not only to the People of Israel in the days of Isaiah, but also throughout history. Try re-reading the Isaiah passage, but think of the Jewish victims of the Holocaust, or the pogroms, or the Inquisition, or the Crusades, or other Christian persecutions of Jews, as you read it. Ask yourself, what violence did these Jews do to deserve the fate given to them by Christians? The answer, of course, is none.

Jesus did not fulfill this "prophecy" of Isaiah 53, nor did he fulfill any of the real and important prophecies concerning the true Messiah.

CHAPTER 15

CONCLUSIONS AND QUESTIONS

There are an increasing number of people who either ignore the differences between Judaism and Christianity or they simply do not know any better. These people make this mistake for a number of reasons.

Many people hear about and use the term, "Judeo-Christian Tradition." Without understanding the term, they make the assumption that the only thing that separates Judaism from Christianity is that one faith believes that Jesus was the messiah while the other does not. They do not understand that some Christians often use "Judeo-Christian Tradition" to refer to the Judaism that preceded Christianity which does not include the Rabbinic Judaism that has defined Judaism for over 2,000 years, and which informs and shapes every branch of Judaism today. They use the term to indicate the origin of Christian beliefs and that culminated in Christianity. Or they use the term "Judeo-Christian Tradition" to refer to those times when there is, indeed, an overlap between Jewish values and ethics and Christian values and ethics.

Another characteristic that leads many to disregard the differences between Judaism and Christianity is that the denomination of Christianity that calls itself Messianic "Judaism" has influenced not only the Conservative and Evangelical Christian denominations, but more and more of the Liberal denominations as well. More and more churches of all denominations are holding Passover seders and celebrating other Jewish holidays like Sukkot, the Feast of Tabernacles. Some Christian weddings are including a Christianized Ketubah, the Jewish marriage contract, while some Christian children are celebrating Christianized Bar and Bat Mitzvahs. Every time Christianity takes a ritual or holiday observance from Judaism, whether they give it a Christian spin or not, they are leading their members and their denominations to believe that Judaism and Christianity are not that different after all, and further blur the lines between the two faiths.

Messianic "Judaism" has also done much to blur the differences between Judaism and Christianity. Heavily supported by Evangelical Christianity, the most fundamental technique of their missionary efforts is to get Jews to believe the false idea that one can be a Jew and a Christian at the same time, that they are not abandoning Judaism when they accept Christian theology and the Christian interpretations of the Hebrew Scriptures. This cannot work unless they dissolve the separations between the two faiths and make it look like everything Christian is to be found rooted in Judaism and Jewish rituals.

Because the best friends of the State of Israel are these very same Evangelical Christians that support missionary efforts to the Jews, members of the Jewish community have a conflict of interest when they emphasize the differences between the two faiths. So as not to risk alienating the support given to the State of Israel by these Christians, Jews will soften their statements that conflict with Christian theology. Rabbis are now calling Jesus a rabbi, when no beit din (court) of rabbis ever gave him smicha (ordination). Jews will emphasize the overlap spoken about above, between Judaism and Christianity regarding values and ethics, over the greater differences that exist theologically, as well as those differences that regard Biblical interpretation.

Jews have grown up believing that Judaism is as good as Christianity, that it is as reasonable, as beneficial, as right and as true as Christianity. By believing that Judaism is only as good as and not better than, more true than, more in consonance with Biblical values than, more beneficial to its adherents than Christianity, then there is no reason to distinguish between the beliefs of the two faiths or to refrain from following a little bit of both. This has worked to justify Jewish assimilation. After all, if the two faiths are the same, if one is as good, as true as the other, then why not be more like the majority? Why maintain differences, much less emphasize them, when one can join the majority, act and believe like the majority, if the minority faith is not more true, more right, more in agreement with Biblical values and beliefs than the faith of the majority?

While the ignorance of the differences between Judaism and Christianity has led some Jews to assimilate or to simply become secular, it also has misled Christians into believing that the only reason why Jews have not converted to Christianity is that the history of Christian antisemitism precludes it. They think that because of the early Church's limitations upon Jews, its suppression of Judaism, that because of the Crusades, the Inquisition (which had more to do with keeping ex-Jews in line with Catholic beliefs than it did with the conversion of Jews), Pogroms, the Holocaust, and other Christian persecutions of Jews, that Jews refuse to convert. These Christians do not understand that the real obstacle to Jewish conversion is the sharp contrast between Christian and Jewish beliefs and assumptions. And so here, too, the differences between Judaism and Christianity must be ignored or suppressed to succeed in Jewish proselytizing.

One cannot have it both ways. Judaism and Christianity disagree on the most fundamental beliefs and theologies of the two faiths. The two faiths believe in diametrically opposite, mutually exclusive things. They cannot both be right. Either God is One and indivisible, or God is a trinity where one "person" in the Godhead is separate and unequal to the other two, but they are all three somehow one and the same. Either God is God and Man is Man and God does not become a man and a man does not become God, or God took on human form in the person of Jesus. Either we are responsible for our choices between Good or Evil or the actions of a Devil is to blame. Either we are born in sin, and are guilty of the sins committed by ancestors and we die as a result, or we are born neutral and our choices between Good and Evil make us what we are. Either, Jewish law was God's loving gift to the Jews to make the Jews better off and to make the world a better place, or God gave the law to teach us that we cannot be anything but sinners. Either one person can die for the sins of another and thereby remove from the other their guilt from their sins, or one person cannot die for the sins of another. Either there is forgiveness and atonement only when there is a blood sacrifice for the sins, or God has given us many ways to obtain forgiveness and atonement. Either God wants and accepts a human sacrifice or God does not want or accept a human sacrifice. Either Jesus was the messiah or he was not. Either Jews define who is a Jew, or ex-Jews who are now Christians and Christians who are Jewish wannabees define who is a Jew. Either the Jewish roots of Christianity are found in the rituals and holidays and Holy Days of Judaism, or Christians are merely "discovering" what they themselves have planted. Either the Jewish understanding of verses in the Hebrew Scriptures and the beliefs they reflect are clear and consistent with other verses, or God has changed His mind and the interpretation by Christianity of those same verses reflects that change.

One can only conclude from the Biblical verses contrasted with verses from the Christians' New Testament in this book, that the theologies of Judaism and Christianity consist of different beliefs and Biblical interpretations that are mutually exclusive, and that the beliefs and interpretations of Christianity are not in agreement with, but are antithetical to, the clear, simple, consistent meaning of the Hebrew Scriptures.

I have laid out for the reader the Biblical verses that indicate what Jews believe and why, and I have contrasted them with verses from the Christian's New Testament that show what Christians believe. I have shown how if the Bible is to be believed, if it is to be accepted as authoritative, then the beliefs of Christianity are contrary to what the Bible clearly, simply, and consistently states. Christians may take verses from the Bible out of context. They can mistranslate them, and they can give them a Christian spin. But if the Christian understanding, however they reach their understanding, is contrary to the Bible, then their beliefs are simply unbiblical and must be rejected by all those who believe in the authority of the Bible.

If the Christian community wishes to cling to their beliefs, that is their choice. But to do so, they must resolve for themselves questions that Jews have asked, and answered, through the millennia.

First and foremost of these questions is, when did God change His mind? If the Bible is clear and consistent, but Christianity holds beliefs that conflict with the Bible, then God must have changed His mind. When did this happen?

If God changed His mind, why didn't God bring together every Jew, as He did at Mt. Sinai, and deliver to them this new Divine revelation?

Why would anyone believe Jesus and the stories about him, if the beliefs about Jesus and the theology of Christianity contradict what we already know from the revelation received by the whole Jewish People together at Mt. Sinai?

Why did God, as the Muslims claim, as the Buddhists claim, and as many other faiths say about their individual founders, why did God give His revelation only to a single person, who then sought out those who would accept his story, and who then went out to proselytize the rest of the world?

The Jews answered these questions long ago, in their rejection of Christian theology as unbiblical, and as this book proves. We were promised by God that God would never break his covenant with us, that it is an eternal covenant as God is the eternal God, and as the Sabbath will eternally be observed by the Jews as the eternal sign of that eternal covenant (Exodus 31:12-17).

For all questions that Christian missionaries have asked of Jews, there has been and will always be a Jewish answer, a valid, reasonable, rational Biblical response. For every Biblical verse that Christian missionaries use to persuade Jews to abandon their ancestral faith, there is a valid, reasonable, rational Jewish interpretation that remains true to values and beliefs that are clear and consistent throughout the Bible.

Christians will never accept the Jewish response to these questions or the Jewish interpretation of our Hebrew Scriptures. They cannot, because to do so would require them to abandon their faith. However, they don't have to, because Judaism never believed that only Jews go to heaven, or that God is so petty that He refuses to answer a sincere prayer prayed to one who is not God.

One must conclude from all that I have shown in this book, in spite of all the forces in our present society to make it appear that all faiths are the same or that we all basically believe the same things, there are differences between Judaism and Christianity. These differences will always remain irreconcilable.

Resources

Introduction to Judaism

Kushner, Rabbi Harold. *To Life: A Celebration of Jewish Being and Thinking.* Warner Books. 1994.

Prager, Dennis and Rabbi Joseph Telushkin, Rabbi Joseph. *The Nine Questions People Ask About Judaism the Intelligent Skeptic's Guide.* Touchstone. 1986.

Telushkin, Rabbi Joseph. *Jewish Literacy: The Most Important Things to Know About the Jewish Religion, Its People, and Its History.* William Morrow. 2008.

Comparative Religion

Berger, David. *The Jewish-Christian Debate in the High Middle Ages: A Critical Edition of the Nizzahon Vetus.* ACLS Humanities. 2008.

Cohen, Arthur A. *The Myth of the Judeo-Christian Tradition.* Schocken Books. 1971.

Fisch, Dov Aharoni. *Jews for Nothing.* Feldheim Publishers. 1984.

Lasker, Daniel J. *Jewish Philosophical Polemics Against Christianity in the Middle Ages.* Littman Library of Jewish Civilization. 2007.

Kaplan, Rabbi Aryeh. *The Real Messiah? A Jewish Response to Missionaries.* The Union of Orthodox Jewish Congregations of America and The National Conference of Synagogue Youth. 1976.

Neusner, Jacob. *Jews and Christians: The Myth of a Common Tradition.* Trinity Press International, Wipf and Stock Publishers. 2012.

Neusner, Jacob. *A Rabbi Talks With Jesus.* McGill-Queen's University Press. 2000.

Schwartzbaum, Aaron and Suzanna Spiro. *Beware of Soul Snatchers: How Jews Can Save Themselves From Missionary Assault.* Ordering Information: http://www.shemayisrael.co.il/orgs/toralife/Book1.html.

Sigal, Gerald. *The Blood Atonement Deception: How Christianity Distorted Biblical Atonement.* Xlibris Corporation. 2010.

Sigal, Gerald. *Trinity Doctrine Error: A Jewish Analysis.* Xlibris Corporation. 2006.

Silver, Abba Hillel. *Where Judaism Differed: An Inquiry Into the Distinctiveness of Judaism.* Jason Aronson. 1989.

Weiss-Rosmarin, Trude. *Judaism and Christianity: The Differences.* Jonathan David Publishing Inc. 1988.

Zakar, Shoshana and Dovid Kaufman. *Judaism Online: Confronting Spirituality on the Internet.* 1998. http://www.jewsforjudaism.org.

Origins of Christianity

Carpenter, Edward. *The Origins of Pagan and Christian Beliefs.* Senate, of Random House, London, UK. 2009.

Cook, Michael J. *Modern Jews Engage the New Testament: Enhancing Jewish Well-Being in a Christian Environment.* Jewish Lights Publishing. 2008.

Festinger, Leon; *et al. When Prophecy Fails.* Martino Fine Books. 2011.

Freke, Timothy and Peter Gandy. *The Jesus Mysteries: Was the "Original Jesus" a Pagan God?* Harmony Books, New York, NY. 2001.

Graves, Kersey. *The World's Sixteen Crucified Saviors: Christianity Before Christ.* Research Associates, Frontline Distribution International, Inc., Chicago. 2011.

Helms, Randel. *Gospel Fictions.* Prometheus Books. 1989.

Maccoby, Hyam. *Judas Iscariot and the Myth of Jewish Evil.* Free Press. 1992.

Maccoby, Hyam. *The Mythmaker: Paul and the Invention of Christianity.* Harper/Collins Publishers. 1998.

Robertson, J.M. *Pagan Christs.* Barnes and Noble, New York, NY Books, 2008.

Prooftexts

Avraham of Troki, Isaac ben. *Faith Strengthened: 1,200 Biblical Refutations to Christian Missionaries*, KTAV Publishing House, Inc.

Drazin, Michoal. *Their Hollow Inheritance: A Comprehensive Refutation of the New Testament and Its Missionaries.* Feldheim Publishing. 1990.

Greenstein, S.J. *We Are Not Going to Burn in Hell.* Biblically Speaking Publishing Co. 2002.

Maccoby, Hyam. *Judaism on Trial: Jewish-Christian Disputations in the Middle Ages.* Littman Library. 1993.

Moshe, Beth. *Judaism's Truth Answers the Missionaries.* Block Publishing Company. New York, NY. 1997.

Sigal, Gerald. *Isaiah 53: Who is the Servant?* Xlibris Corporation..

Sigal, Gerald. The Jew and the Christian Missionary: A Jewish Response to Missionary Christianity. KTAV Publishing House, Inc. 1981.

Sigal, Gerald. *Anti-Judaism in the New Testament.* Xlibris Corporation. 2004

Singer, Tovia. *Let's Get Biblical! Why Doesn't Judaism Accept the Christian Messiah?* RNBN Publishers. "Let's Get Biblical!" A complete 24-part CD series. 2010.

Autobiographies

Carmel, Abraham. *So Strange My Path: A Spiritual Pilgrimage.* Bloch Publishing. 1997.

Kamentsky, Ellen. *Hawking God: A Young Jewish Woman's Ordeal in Jews for Jesus.* Saphire Press, 1992.

Mordechai, Tova. *To Play With Fire: One Woman's Remarkable Odyssey.* Urim Publications. 2002.

Scalamonti, John David. *Ordained To Be A Jew: A Catholic Priest's Conversion to Judaism.* KTAV Publishing House. 1992.

Schachnowitz, Selig. *Avrohom Ben Avrohom.* Feldheim Publishers. 1978.

Sherman, Shlomoh. *Escape From Jesus: One Man's Search for a Meaningful Judaism.* Decalogue Books, 1986.

Taylor, Penina. *Coming Full Circle: A Jewish Woman's Journey Through Christianity and Back.* Hatikva Books. 2009.

Websites

JewsForJudaism.CA
JewsForJudaism.org
OutreachJudaism.org
The Jewish Israel Bookstore at: http://astore.amazon.com/jewiisra-20
http://www.virtualyeshiva.com/counter-index.html
http://judaismsanswer.com/apologetics.htm
http://FaithStrengthened.org
http://www.sapphire.com/hawking

INDEX OF BIBLICAL AND CHRISTIAN NEW TESTAMENT VERSES

NUMBERS
1:2—88
5:6-7—67
15:22—64
15:24-29—64
15:30-31—65
15:32-36—65
16:47—61
23:19—8
31:50—61

DEUTERONOMY
4:29—67
6:3—39
6:4—1
6:9—26
6:4-9—32
11:13-21—40
12:30-31—72
14:24-26—194
22:8—25
24:16—19; 51; 126; 172; 186
29:29—174
30:11-14—36

I SAMUEL
15:1—82
15:29—8
16:13—82
16:23—4

II SAMUEL
7:12-17—89

I KINGS
8:38-39—69

MALACHI
    4:5-6—93; 165

PSALMS
    19:7—144
    19:7-9—174
    34:14—67
    34:18—67
    40:6—68
    40:8—174
    51:1—140
    51:16-17 –68
    89:20-27—180
    105:6-10—169
    106:37-38—73
    109:6-7—13
    110:1—176
    111:7-8—175

PROVERBS
    10:2—61
    11:4—62
    16:6—62
    21:3—62
    28:13—68
    30:2-4—178
    30:18-20—135

JOB
    1:1—36
    2:3-6—12
    33:26—67
    33:26-28—70

ECCLESIASTES
    12:7—14; 152

18:19—3
18:31-34—54; 188
19:27—165; 195
22:35—166
22:36—195
23:26-27—190
23:34—2

JOHN
1:19-21—94
1:29—74
2:15—193
3:36—56
6:35—121
12:11—191
12:42—192
14:28—3
18:22-23—162; 192
20:1-2—147
20:17—164

ACTS
16:31—27

ROMANS
3:19-24—29
3:20-24—33
3:28—33
6:23—38
10:6-9—36

1 CORINTHIANS
9:20-22—117
15:21-22—18